€6-

THEONAS

THEONAS

CONVERSATIONS OF A SAGE

BY

JACQUES MARITAIN

TRANSLATED BY F. J. SHEED

SHEED & WARD
LONDON AND NEW YORK
1933

FIRST PUBLISHED MARCH 1933

PRINTED AT THE WHITEFRIARS PRESS
LONDON AND TONBRIDGE
FOR SHEED & WARD
31 PATERNOSTER ROW, E.C.4

CONTENTS

PREFACE TO THE ENGLISH EDITION

THIS work was composed a dozen years ago. Its intention, or part of its intention, was frankly polemic. I wished to help towards the extermination of certain prejudices, hoary by now and dusty with age, of the modern ideology, which I held to be serious obstacles to the progress of the spirit. Reading over again these pages of the past, I feel how incomplete they are: yet I think they may still have their utility, for the prejudices against which they 'fight have not quite managed to die.

The trouble about works of controversy is that often the author—particularly when he yields to the wicked pleasure of baiting some of his readers—tends unwittingly to express only one of the aspects of his thought. The first editions of *Theonas* apparently suffered from this defect, since certain passages led honest critics to hold the author as an incorrigible reactionary, a man committed to hostility towards modern physics, and—more scandalous still—towards Progress.

Shall I ever get them to see differently? Shall I ever get them to grasp that in my opinion it is to Thomism alone that the privilege belongs of reconciling metaphysics and the natural sciences? That Thomism alone is an essentially progressive philosophy, loves movement while holding stability in honour, gives us an exact sense of the renewals necessary in human things? And may I add that, to my thinking, it contains germinative energies potent enough to burst asunder the super-annuated framework of " bourgeois " and " anti-bourgeois " thought ?

In conclusion may I say that, on some of the problems touched upon in *Theonas*, I have stated my mind more fully in other works published since then—*Primauté du Spirituel*,* *Religion et Culture*,† *Les Degrés du Savoir ;* and that this English translation has been made from a revised text, in which, by the inclusion of corrections and additions prepared for the forthcoming French edition, certain misconstructions are obviated. I should like to thank Mr. Sheed for all the care he has taken over the work of translation.

J. M.

December, 1932.

* *The Things that are not Caesar's* (Sheed & Ward).
† *Religion and Culture* (Sheed & Ward).

THE FREEDOM
OF THE INTELLECT

THE FREEDOM OF THE INTELLECT

ON an April morning in 1920, as I was strolling by the Place de la Sorbonne, I met my old friend Philonous. He was on his way back from Geneva, and, with a suit-case in his hand, was studying the mottos which adorn the statue of Auguste Comte : Order and Progress. He seemed to be meditating upon their relevance.

He has travelled a good deal since the death of Hylas, and I have at home some letters from him—not many, and received at long intervals—which show that he has not ceased to follow, enthusiastically if not professionally, the movement of philosophic ideas in all countries. There he stood, young, eager and handsome, with the same China blue eyes and the same nobly idealistic brow—scarcely changed, in fact, since the days when he was hovering round Bishop Berkeley.* It was at the Bishop's house that I last saw him, the best part of two hundred years ago. In those days he called himself an *Immaterialist*, and was much concerned about the preparation of tar-water. . . .

As I approached, he swung round, all excitement, and said : " I wish you would help me to solve a problem that is worrying me : how is it possible that intelligent men, men who are always acclaiming the primacy of the intellect, seem at this moment—at any rate in France— to be proposing what is really the intellect's enslavement ?

* See Bishop Berkeley's *Three Dialogues between Hylas and Philonous.*

3   B 2

In their eyes the intellect has no higher purpose than to serve. They want it to surrender its independence and work like a paid assistant in the service of this, that or the other truth that seems to them vital. Some of them—and I am told they have your approval—are actually striving to bring back philosophy to the discipline of the School—and even (though this sounds a sheer impossibility) to revive the outworn problems of theology! Others in season and out of season repeat that 'the intellect must not, at any cost, hold itself dispensed from service.' Yet surely your own Aristotle held that intellect is at the apex of being : that it must not serve but be served."

" It may be," I replied, " that Aristotle and you have not quite the same notion of what intellect is, and I fancy that all your difficulties arise from a failure to grasp his meaning. But, leaving that for a moment, what about yourself? Surely, now that you have become a Bergsonian, you do not rate the intellect so very high ? "

" I value it for the pleasures it gives us ; apart from that, I think it is not of much use save to turn men into mathematicians and—if they take it for a sun when it is no more than a dark lantern—to ensnare them in the illusion called metaphysics. . . . But how do you know that my sympathies are at the moment tending in M. Bergson's direction ? My last letter told you of my admiration for M. Maine de Biran, to whom I had just been introduced ; that is a good hundred years ago, and since that time you have heard no word from me."

" It was easy enough to guess. The inner soul of your philosophy is, you will agree, the postulate that the mind of man acts as a pure spirit and knows as the angels know, transcending the labour both of abstraction and of step-by-step reasoning. To begin with, you believed that such a mode of knowledge was possible to the human intellect. In those days you followed Plato, till you gave him up for Descartes and Malebranche. Then you divided your—I will scarcely say allegiance—between your great friend Berkeley, whose writings spread your name so widely, and Leibnitz. But as the years went by, when Kant had persuaded you that the intellect could know only what it had itself created and that the absolute was altogether beyond its reach, there was but one possibility for you. That contact with the Absolute which you had given up hoping from the intellect, you could look for only in the Bergsonian intuition, the *sentiment de la vie* or some similar development of imaginative sympathy. That, roughly, is the process by which the *anti*-intellectualism of to-day—or rather of yesterday—comes—or came—to be the normal issue of the exaggerated intellectualism and rationalism of the day before."

" I am delighted to hear you affirm that the philosophy of pure change is the present-day fruit of a long and unbroken effort of thought. What you say is some compensation for the insult so often hurled at modern philosophers that they lack all historic tradition."

" But there is a great difference between the ' tradition ' of the moderns and the tradition of the *philosophia perennis*. Modern philosophies grow out of what has gone before, but rather by way of contradiction : the scholastics by way of agreement and further development. The result is that philosophy in our days is like a series of episodes simply stuck end to end, not like a tree where each is organically related to each and all to the roots. But given all that, I grant you that even those who hold it to be the primary duty of every thinker worth his salt to give men a *new* conception of the universe, cannot, in fact, advance a step or set forth their discoveries without making use of the results of those who have gone before them ; so true is it that the labour of the mind, by its very nature, demands a collaboration running through the years.

" Thus in their criticism of the intellect, Bergson and Le Roy were merely elaborating into a theory the consequences of a state of mind which *in practice* had long reigned among ' intellectuals.' From beginning to end of the nineteenth century, these men, or at any rate the more misguided of them, professed by their way of acting—*in actu exercito* as we should say—that the intellect has only a subjective and relative value : that enclosed in itself and safely padlocked in its *cogito*, independent of all objective measure, it can do nought save take its pleasure in the thousand scintillations of its own excellence, like a god amusing himself with dreams. For them the exercise of the intelligence could be no more than a game, a luxury, a spare time occupation not for busy men—what Kant called a ' finality without end.' Free ? In reality the intellect—thus twisted from its true line by the worship of brute fact, made subordinate to sensation, harnessed in the service of industry by that utilitarian and earth-bound science which reached its highest or lowest level in Germany—was in servitude to the inferior powers of the human creature. Hence the wearing down, so often noticed, of that faculty—driven to a fury of activity, but no longer acting towards its natural end, and bearing no fruit since it was uprooted from that world of objective

6

being, independent of itself, which is the only soil from which it may draw life.

" It is against such a use, arising from such a notion, of the intellect that the phrases which puzzle you so deeply are directed : that is why they aim at setting the intellect of man to the service of the good of man. And in that you will find the true meaning of the mind's " leisure "— its totally free, because totally disinterested, activity. To-day this has become, at any rate temporarily, impossible : because, in the universal peril, all that is most sacred in man—including, therefore, the very life of the mind—absolutely demands the mobilisation of all the powers of man's soul.

" You remember that curious dialogue set down by M. Chevrillon in his admirable study of Chesterton :

" ' But, M. Taine, how do you save the world ? ' asked an Englishwoman—in a loud voice—at a dinner at which the author of the *Notes sur l'Angleterre* happened to be.

" ' My *dear* madam, I do *not* save the world,' replied M. Taine."

" That," interjected Philonous, " is because M. Taine was not English."

" Also because he did not live in the twenties of this century. To-day all of us, great workmen and little, must ' labour with God ' for the salvation of the world, work with every fibre of our being for the common good of all men. . . . And yet only ruin can come of it if we call upon the intellect to abdicate its rights, to give up its freedom and the leisure—in the sense I have already described—which God intended it to have."

" Here, stop ! " burst in Philonous, thoroughly worked

7

up, " you're going too fast. How can you speak of the liberty of the intellect and the leisure of the intellect ? When you propose to use it entirely in practical action and to have it working without respite for the common good ? "

" That is the precise point of your misconception," I answered. " I said that the intellect must work for the common good of the world and of humanity ; I never said that it must be used only in practical action. I said that the false liberty and false leisure of an intellect purely egoist, subjectivist, quietist, have had their day ; I never said that the true liberty and the true leisure of the intellect have had their day, for their day is eternal. The one question is to know *how* the intellect works for the common good. But to answer that question, it is necessary to go into certain details concerning the nature of the intellect, and I must ask you to grant me a moment's patience."

" Very well, I give in. Only for heaven's sake let us sit down. Here is a bench. . . ."

" There are two things especially to be considered in the intellect," I began. " First of all its action is alto- gether *immanent*, as we call it : by that we mean that its nature is not to produce a term external to itself, but only to perfect in *quality* the knowing mind, which in the very act of knowing *becomes*, after a certain manner, the things that it knows : it " becomes " them (even though they are material) *immaterially*—or in scholastic language *inten- tionally*—by making them participate in the spirituality of the intellect : but it does not become them *really* or *materially* by becoming absorbed and losing its identity in them, as for instance M. Bergson's ' intuition ' would

8

have us believe. This immanence, which is the property of life as life, is a characteristic essential to the intellect as intellect.

" Secondly, in this vital operation of knowing, our intelligence is *dependent* upon some object not itself. It is not a mere subjective game : on the contrary, it is an act of subjection and submission to the object known ; for whereas the intelligence of *God* is both the cause and the measure of the truth of things, things are both the cause and the measure of the truth of *our* intelligence ; and it is precisely in this act of subjection to the object that its liberty consists. It is made for *being*, it is in its totality reaching out towards the object, towards the other *as* other ; it needs the dominating contact of the object, but only that it may be enriched by it—in a victorious action which springs from its own living spontaneity, from its *autonomy*. For, as it does itself immaterially become the object, it is truly from itself that the act of knowing emanates, which perfects it—though from itself thus become the *other*, fertilised by being, rightly subjected to the real. That is what Kant did not see and what St. Thomas saw very clearly. Kant had a profound feeling of the spontaneity of the intellectual nature, but because he believed that the act of knowing consists in *creating* the other, not in *becoming* the other, he foolishly reversed the order of dependence between the object of knowledge and the human intellect and made the human intellect the measure and law of the object."

" What conclusions do you draw from all this ? "

" The first conclusion I draw—though only in parenthesis—is this, that since the *immanent* activity of our intellect is essentially *dependent* upon the object, there is

9

neither repose nor happiness for it save when it is totally conquered (that is, convinced) and mastered by the object, because then only is it truly free because following the nature of its own activity.

"These considerations may perhaps make clear to you how discipline—whether the discipline of the faith and of theology, the philosophic discipline of the School, the mere discipline of rule and measure in the Arts—leads not to the enslavement, but on the contrary to the spontaneous flowering, of the intellect and its fullest freedom. For the intellect, when it believes on the witness of the apostles, is in submission not to this witness but to God Himself, by the interior light of faith. When it learns from a master the truth of science, it is in submission not to this master, but actually to being, by the interior light of rational evidence. When in its activity it has conformed to the rules of right reason, it is in submission, not to the regulations of men, but to the demands of the object, of the work to be done, by the interior light of the technique of the art in question. And the more it is thus in submission, the less does it suffer constraint."

"Your parenthesis, as you call it, has lasted quite long enough. What you set out to tell me was how the intellect may work best for the common good of man."

"But don't you see that we have already answered the question? If the liberty of the intellect were simply a claim to have no end other than its own satisfaction, in total independence of the hard but salutary domination of the object—it might seem that the service of the common good would be equivalent to an abdication of its liberty and a renouncing of that which constitutes its happiness, in subordination to the interests of action.

But if there is no true liberty for the intellect save in submission to the object, if there is no true leisure for it save in the activity of knowing the object, then it is obvious that it will best serve the common interests of men precisely in assuring its own leisure and its own liberty, precisely in working *disinterestedly*—which means not simply that it may take pleasure in its own operation, but that it may be subjected to that which *is*. For men are nourished by being ; as their body lives by bread, their mind lives by being, by truth, by beauty ; they have a measureless need of a constantly renewed inpouring of these transcendentals. By the mere fact of applying itself to being, the intellect works for the good both of the City and of the universe.

" If we do not always grasp this, it is because we live most obviously in the senses and find a difficulty in representing to ourselves an activity which does not consist in producing something external, but which, being of an order superior to matter, remains and finds its completion in itself. Nevertheless, the immanent act of knowing—like the act of loving which depends upon it— has a life. Better, it *is* life, life *par excellence*.

" It is of vital importance that there should be men who bend all their intellectual powers to the immediate welfare of the City : it would be a meanness in us to repay them with ingratitude. But it is also of vital importance that there should be men who bend all their intellectual powers simply and solely towards *being*— whether towards its contemplation inasmuch as being is truth, or towards the production of works of art inasmuch as being is beauty. We should delight in their leisure— their freedom, that is, from occupations of more immediate utility—for it is necessary to the City, and we should demand that it be respected by a world eaten into by the barbarism of the immediately useful : whether they are poets, or philosophers, artists or scholars, they are guarding a sacred thing."

"You mean," said Philonous, "that they cut themselves off from all the interests of men and refuse the service of their labour to any interest other than that of pure intellect ? "

"Certainly not. That would be treating them as half-men or gods, whereas they are men like others. If they hold that their wisdom or their art is the sovereign good, they are idolators, and, at the end of all things, fools. God is divinity, but the artist is not art, and the philosopher is not philosophy. As *men*, they can have and must have other ends than the end proper to their art or their philosophy taken in itself. All that is asked of them, in order that they may not be unfaithful to the supreme disinterestedness of the intellect and the purity of its discipline, is this : that whatever may be their ultimate intentions and the passions that they have at heart, they should direct the immediate operation of their minds only according to the demands of the truth to be known or the object to be created. But if love does not set them to the work, the chances are that the work will be mediocre or merely futile."

"In other words," said Philonous, rising, "you claim to be equally removed from the way of Renan and from pragmatism—from a view of the mind which makes its own pleasure its only rule as from that utilitarianism that spurns the mind altogether."

"Both these philosophies derive, as it seems to me, from

the same self-worshipping perversion of thought—and they are equally worthy of detestation. One man takes the created intellect as its own last end ; another essentially subordinates the intellect to practical action ; both of them offend against the true nature of the intellect and twist the human being from its true line. We must firmly grasp that it is only by considering the object, only by restoring the objective value of our powers of knowing, that we can escape from both these vices : so that we shall at once prevent the intellectuals from using the intellect against the good of man, and maintain in its fullness Aristotle's great idea of the royal liberty of the intellect."

" This great idea of yours seems to be pretty well forgotten by our contemporaries."

" Which does not prove that it is false. But so far we have merely scratched the surface. Really to dig into it, we should have to discuss the theory—Aristotle's theory —of the Superman."

" Well, at any rate we shall not discuss it to-day. Here comes the rain."

Thereupon we separated. Philonous made his way to the " Bank of Philosophic Constructions and of the Exchange of Ideas," where he had a large cheque to cash.

THE THEORY
OF THE SUPERMAN

THE THEORY OF THE SUPERMAN

FOLLOWING upon our first discussion, Philonous asked me for some further explanation concerning Aristotle and the Superman. We decided, therefore, to go together to consult a friend of mine, a solitary, much more able than I to satisfy him. He is a man not only very wise but very pious, deeply learned in the philosophy of the Schoolmen, but rather odd in his appearance. His name is Theonas.

"And why," Philonous asked me, "did your friend choose this slightly unusual name?"

"In honour of the Abbot Theonas whose story he read in Cassian. This saintly old man, who lived in Lower Egypt, had been married in his youth ; but having one day heard the Abbot John speak of man's duty of leaving all things for God, he made no bones about leaving his wife and went off to the desert to live a life of perfection. My friend, who in all things loves sudden solutions—and who had, furthermore, read of some similar incident in the life of the blessed Lullus, another great eccentric dear to his heart—was pleased to take to himself the name of that holy father. To be quite honest, I fancy that a certain dislike of women had something to say to his choice."

We found Theonas in his garden, a rough pipe in his mouth, busying himself with the careful pruning of a strange tree, whose leaves, very few and very long, and arranged with a most impressive regularity, bore each a word in Latin.

"I am giving some attention," he said, "to the tree of Porphyry which is badly neglected these days by so many gardeners ; they no longer care for genera and species : transformism has muddled them all up. I have here certain rare specimens. Here, for instance "—and he pointed to a stump *very* dried up—" you see the trees planted by Raymond Lully—the elementary tree, the imaginal tree, the impersonal tree, the tree of forty-nine flowers whereon are written the virtues create and increate. . . . There was a time when sages rested in their shade. Further on I have the tree of Descartes which has metaphysics for root, physics for trunk, and medicine, mechanics and ethics for branches ; it yields a little fruit, but bitter . . ."

"Sir," replied Philonous, "we are hoping that you will be kind enough to speak to us a little on Aristotle's doctrine of the Superman. It seems that you live in a certain familiarity with that philosopher. Personally until yesterday I thought that the Superman had been invented by Nietzsche."

"A great error, dear Sir," replied Theonas. "All peoples and all founders of moral systems—except Confucius, of course—have sought to achieve the Super-man. The legends of heroes, the demi-gods of the ancients, their wise men, all show this clearly enough. The actual word 'superman' was used for the first time, I fancy, by St. Gregory the Great when he said that 'those who have wisdom in divine things are, as it were, supermen.' [1] The only point about the Superman that

[1] Notes are at the end o the volume.

was left for the feeble-mindedness of modern times to conceive, was that he should be the product of an historic evolution, beginning with Haeckel's *Bathybius,* rising through the monkey to man, and one day, apparently, to rise from man to some still greater animal. Whereas, in fact, the desire of the very deepest part of our moral being is for a man who *remains man* and who yet surpasses the level of humanity."

" Wherein, then, lies the originality of Aristotle ? "

" Aristotle understood *in what manner* man may surpass the level of humanity. He understood that the principle of this elevation cannot be found in the human *subject :* how could one find in *man* that whereby the level of man might be surpassed ? This principle of elevation, then, can be sought only in the *object*—something not man, with which men may yet come into contact—provided that this object should itself be superhuman : in other words, it must be sought in something other than man and nobler than man, to which he may adhere and which may thus raise him above himself. And how can man thus make contact with, and adhere to, the object ? By his intellect.

" Practical activity, prudence, the moral virtues, which render the human subject perfectly proportioned in activity to the ends of his nature, are all things essentially human : too human, alas ! They leave man—where they find him—in human life. If he *can* attain to a life above the human, the first movement of his attainment can be only by the speculative intellectual virtues, by the activity of contemplation which transports him into—all but merges him in—the object and thus bears him above the level of human life. The Superman, as Aristotle

C 2

saw him, was the sage speculating on the things of eternity.

" You see then how decisively the intellectualism of Aristotle is opposed in this to every subjectivist or merely immanentist tendency. Which, doubtless, is one of the reasons why Luther and all the apostles of the Ego instinctively dislike him. St. Thomas, on the other hand, when he treats of the perfect life and of contemplation, remains strictly faithful to all the formal principles of Aristotle. Nowhere can one better see how the thought of the Greek philosopher can be transfigured without being altered, by the superior light of that plane on to which theology elevates it. Christian contemplation, which is supernatural and the fruit of virtues which directly unite the soul to the inmost life of the Divinity, is a very different thing from contemplation as Aristotle saw it : yet, in fact, grace does no more than reduplicate, lifted to its own level, a relation already given in the natural order : in other words, it is still *by the object* that man is raised above himself and placed in the way of perfection. And now consider the Stoics. They derive from the cynics whose model was Hercules."

" And whose wisdom," interjected Philonous, " might be called the wisdom of Muscle."

" Quite so," said Theonas, " whereas according to Aristotle, men of softer flesh are naturally more fitted than other man for the works of the intellect and hence for wisdom."

" Thomas Aquinas, for example," I said. " To say nothing of yourself, my dear Theonas, with your suggestion of some gorgeous Rembrandt burgomaster turned hermit. The idea pleases me. It explains why

Rodin's muscular Thinker seems to be having so much trouble with his thinking; looks, in fact, as though he were bracing himself to an effort contrary to his nature."

Theonas wasted no time on me.

"The Stoics," he went on, "as opposed to Aristotle are, from our present point of view, subjectivists : they seek the principle of the Superman's life in that which is of its own nature human, in moral virtue. To achieve the Superman, they have therefore to use violence and overstrain their virtue. But though they may swell and swell, stretch and strain, harden and stiffen their bodies, they can become inhuman, they cannot elevate themselves to a life really surpassing the life of man. Therefore they doubted whether a truly wise man could be found upon the earth."

PHILONOUS. So do I. But are you sure that you are right in saying that Aristotle held the life of contemplation to be a superhuman life ? Was it not rather for him the life of man most fully man ?

THEONAS. It would be better to say that for him it was both at once ; and it is precisely in this that he seems to me to have seen most deeply into our nature. Notice what he says in the first and the tenth book of the *Ethics*. If our felicity consists primarily in the activity of contemplation, it is not solely because this activity considered in itself is life *par excellence*, life at its most stable and most delectable, conferring the greatest measure of independence or αὐτάρχεια, and bearing with it the " leisure " of supreme possession. It is also because, considered in relation to our species, it responds to the most specifically human of man's operations, namely the operation of the intellect. Yet to live the contemplative life is to live according to the mode of pure spirits : to live the life of pleasure is to live according to the mode of the beasts ; and to live the active social life is to live according to the mode of men ; and we are " slaves in so many respects " that wisdom, that is to say metaphysical or theological contemplation, cannot for us be a good, possessed wholly and entirely as our own.

This apparent antinomy is explained by the very nature of the rational animal. That by which man is most truly man is the intellect, which in him is something divine, and by which he participates in the nature of spirits. A life proportioned to that which is thus the principal thing in man will therefore be a life which *in its perfection* exists only amongst spirits : while the life proper to man, the life according to the human mode, is a less noble life proportioned not to what is highest in our composite essence, but to that composite essence itself. Thus the effort towards heroism, the hope of overpassing the limitations of human life, has its root in the very nature of man, so that it is a betrayal of human nature to persuade men to ' know only what is human, mortals to know only mortal things ' : it is towards the immortal and the divine that human nature must reach out. Thus the sage, though he remains truly man, lives a life better than the purely human life : *Vita quæ est secundum speculationem est melior quam quæ secundum hominem.*

And notice : everything is for the contemplative—the moral virtues are there to procure him interior peace, the whole government of civil life to assure him the exterior peace that he needs ; so that all the functions of human life, since they find their end only in his leisure, would seem to be for his service. After all, does he not appear as dominating the life of society like a veritable superman ? Even were he to limit himself always to the contemplation of truth, communicating nothing to man, he would yet quite well serve the common good from the sole fact that by him human nature attains its end, and that in him the human City produces its noblest fruit.

PHILONOUS. There you have the pagan cult of aristocracy in all its fratricidal harshness ! *Humanum paucis vivit genus.* How can you, being a Christian, hear such a doctrine uttered without indignation ?

THEONAS. You know, of course, that the Christians will soon be the only ones to maintain the privileges of the intellect. The supremacy accorded by a St. Thomas to the aristocracy of the intellect is much purer and more magnanimous *because* more humble, than that of a Goethe or a Nietzsche or even an Aristotle. But it is fraternal, and not in him fratricidal—it is *for* the brotherhood, not against it. Further, I must admit that in the last point I made, I insisted too exclusively perhaps on what is only an aspect of Aristotle's thought. In truth the philosopher clearly intends that in the perfect man there should be a union of the active with the contemplative life—since he demands for felicity not only contemplation but also, as a necessary means thereto, the exercise of the moral virtues and even the possession of such exterior goods as are requisite. The heroic life, which he opposes to the bestial, is at once contemplation and activity. And he teaches that when, in a human City, there appears a mighty one surpassing in wisdom and in virtue all the members of the City, a superman, a man who among the others is as a god—though such a man, according to the rules of democratic cities, must be put to death or at any rate ostracized as constituting by his very superiority a public danger and as being no longer a citizen—yet according to the rules of absolute justice he should be made King of the City. [2]

PHILONOUS. So there is no middle way for the Superman ? He must be exterminated by his fellow-men or raised to be king.

THEONAS. This, by analogy, is the condition of all superiority among men, and Aristotle had the courage to see it clearly and to say it. When the God-Man came among His own, is it not true that one day a few simple men wished to make Him King—He fled then alone into the mountains—and that at the end, the chief-priests and the guardians of the City put Him to death upon a cross outside the City gates ?

But now I come to a generalization which may possibly satisfy you. Aristotle is a pure philosopher : he establishes the theory of what we call ' pure nature.' But the state of pure nature, as a fact and in the concrete, has never existed for man, who is always found either in the state of grace—that is super-nature—or in the state of *fallen* nature. In so far as man is concerned, many of the problems that Aristotle left and had to leave unsolved, find their solution—just as many of the principles that he formulated find their true value—only in a higher order, of whose existence he had not the least suspicion. The true supermen are the saints : true contemplation is not that of Aristotle, for it presupposes grace and the love of God.

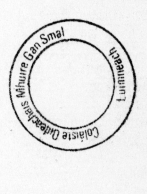

THE INTELLECT AND
THE REIGN OF THE HEART

THE INTELLECT AND THE REIGN OF THE HEART

AFTER a few moments' silence during which, had we been more detached metaphysicians, we might have been able to perceive what M. Bergson calls[3] the *ronron continu de la vie profonde*. Philonous resumed :

" I find it rather odd that you, a solitary, should find a relation between the saints of Christianity and Aristotle's wise men. For a long time now I have been interested in sanctity. I began to study the question when I was taking my first steps in experimental psychology. In particular I was trying to formulate analytically—by the use of Mosso's swing-bed and of Marey's sphygmograph— the connection between religious ideation and blood-pressure. Unfortunately, repeated advertisements in various religious sheets and two or three ecclesiastical reviews had no result : do what I might, I could not procure a supply of the saints that my laboratory needed. Since then I have come to realise the radical insufficiency of quantitative methods and even of conceptual analysis in general—though I attach all the consideration it deserves to psycho-analysis, which so neatly simplifies the problem with its explanation of the whole of man as so many manifestations of Desire ; nor do I neglect the sociological explanation which makes of sanctity a kind of introverted magic ; then, of course, there is the penetrating mystical psychology of the wise and broad-minded Delacroix. . . ."

THEONAS.   Who is he ?

PHILONOUS.   A Professor at the Sorbonne.

THEONAS.   He is a thinker, a metaphysician ?

PHILONOUS.   No, no, a kind of chemist.   If you knew how patiently he decomposes the mystics ; he knows them as if he had made them : it is, in fact, a little depressing, for they lose all their poetic interest.   And at the same time he has an absolutely irreproachable respect for their good faith—at least equal to that of Père Poulain, the famous Catholic specialist.   M. Delacroix is as respectful as an undertaker with a good connection.   And then he has found the name, the scientific, psychological, pheno-menological name—the name without which no metho-dical investigation could possibly set sail !

THEONAS.   What name is that ?

PHILONOUS.   " Theopathic state," my dear Sir.   There. You have it.   *Pati divina*—that phrase already existed, but it needed to be turned into the language of science.   With a name like that, mysticism enters definitively upon its positive phase.   It becomes a legitimate branch of psychology.

THEONAS.   Theopathology ?

PHILONOUS.   A most excellent word, my dear Hermit. I must remember it.   Yet this analysing of his does not give me complete satisfaction.   I do not minimise its importance, but I see in it only an introduction, the anti-chamber to truth, as Leibnitz would have said. It is in the new philosophy—in William James and Bergson—that I seek a theory of that psychosis that you call sanctity.

But still. . . . I do not say that I have arrived at the fullness of light. You know as well as I that on moral questions the Bergsonians are, at the moment, in a rather painful state of uncertainty ; their philosophy is, in its essence, a perpetual renewal, so that no one can, with sufficient authority, foresee in what will consist the ethic foreshadowed by M. Bergson : and our poor old world is so appallingly in need of it ! Yet it seems to me that some of his disciples are not altogether unfaithful to the spirit of his doctrine. Such a one is Noël Vesper, whose *Essai sur la Malléabilite du Monde* [4] I have just read. These men are convinced that existence is action, *élan*, movement : that as a consequence we are not made to rest in God, but always to aspire to Him, never to possess Him : " We shall never attain Him, or rather we must wish to go beyond Him without pausing in Him ; for the state of balance of the meeting, at the point of meeting, would be the immobility of monism." They are further convinced that the need of acting must have forced God to run the " risk " of creating : and this, they say, is a sacrifice by which He gains in moral value. And so they declare, like the American pluralists, for an ethic based upon the notion of risk, of productivity, of action without limit. As Noël Vesper writes : " I lay upon myself the obligation to make myself always stronger in personality, that I may be the better able to make my impress. I feel that I *am* only on condition that I distinguish myself. . . ."

THEONAS. The ego *is* not till it has affirmed itself, as dear old Fichte said !

PHILONOUS (*continuing to read*). " It is the principle of vanity in inferior natures ; of ambition and originality in the great. . . . All rebels are right in the first movement of their revolt. . . .

I shall then be more myself and better myself if I present myself to the world as new and unique. . . . Space, or I stifle ! . . . For us the winds of the limitless ether ! Will you condemn me if, in pursuit of the ideal, I have stumbled, I have left behind me. . . . Ah ! Duties ? They are no longer such if I see greater. I call God to witness that I am innocent of my errors and pure of my faults if I have been blinded with light."

THEONAS. I find a pleasant savour in this cry from the heart, distant echoes of Luther and Rousseau coming to die, mingled with the honeyed notes of the new philosophy. So that is how you conceive the ethic of the *élan vital* ?

PHILONOUS. Yes—at any rate until the publication of that work on Ethics that M. Bergson is now preparing.* Must one say, like the young Bergsonian whom I met at M. Séailles' lecture, that " Morality is a dance which

---

* Since the first edition of this book (1921), the work of M. Bergson here alluded to as in preparation has appeared with the title *Les deux Sources de la Morale et de la Religion* (Paris, 1932). In this matter of the problem of action and contemplation it seems that M. Bergson, as an effect of his own spiritual movement, succeeds in transcending the tendencies to a " mysticism of action " which are logically implied in his philosophy. I cannot see, however, that these tendencies have been altogether eliminated. Cf. Etienne Borne *Spiritualité bergsonienne et spiritualité chrétienne* (Etudes Carmélitaines, October, 1932).

consists in threading one's way across all the forms of becoming without ever stopping at any " ? One thing, at least, seems to me quite clear : namely that in actual fact, moral heroism or sanctity lies in action, in creative energy, not in contemplation, which should be left to the Quietists and the Buddhists. The saints are, above all, mighty *makers*, men of action, who have concentrated all their energies towards this single end, to add to the force of their own personality and to do good to humanity by that supreme form of risk and of creative impulse which we call "sacrifice." Surely Catholics themselves will come to this conception in spite of their tendency to the passive virtues. The canonization of Joan of Arc made me very hopeful in this direction ; though the hope was a little dimmed by the canonization of Margaret Mary Alacoque.

THEONAS. From the beginning, my dear Sir, you have poured out a whole stream of temerarious propositions, but this last I really must take up. You are wildly wrong in seeing these two saints as opposites. The work of one is but the completion of the work of the other. Joan, as you remember, made a gift to the King of Heaven, in due form, of this holy realm which Charles VII. held only in stewardship. Margaret Mary made known to France the demands and the desires of the Heart of that Sovereign King. Both then were messengers of the divine polity. Besides that, you must not forget that Joan of Arc was a mystic no less than Margaret Mary. Everything in her proceeded from the secret illumination of virtues from above, and she died that she might not be unfaithful to the revelations of her Voices, that she might bear witness to the liberty of God's good pleasure, commanding what it wishes to whom it wishes—and thereby giving so much scandal to those proud doctors, *clercs et gens en ce connoissant*, who mistook themselves for the Church.

To return now to the principal point of our discussion—it is not unreasonable to think that upon the matter of sanctity you would have found it more profitable to consult the saints themselves and Catholic theology rather than William James and the new philosophy. St. Thomas would have reminded you that the activity, the energy, of which, carried away by the verbal imaginings of the Pragmatist writers, you spoke a moment ago, is the least noble form of activity : for they are *transitive* action, action by which a being perfects itself only by giving actuality to others, and by, as it were, issuing forth from itself. It strikes the senses more vividly, because its place is the world of material bodies, and its manifestation is by motion : but it is as much diminution as perfection. Action at its highest is *immanent* action, the action of thought and of love, proper to perfect living beings and dwelling in them as a pure quality, bearing witness to the independence of their essence. It is the activity of Him who *is* His own action as He is His own existence, Who knows Himself in His own essence and so loves Himself, Who creates only by super-abundance, in absolute freedom, while yet the production of things adds nothing to His perfection. St. Thomas would also have reminded you that the moral virtues are primarily only *means*, conditions or dispositions necessary that men may arrive at that contemplation of God, which is commenced here below but finds its consummation only in our Father's House and he would have reminded you, also, that if the saints are, as you say, mighty makers, if they acquire a richer personality, are supreme among the benefactors of men, it is because they are fixed in God, united immediately to Him, by the unending gaze of love. As the holy abbot said whose name I bear, " compared with contemplation, the merits and all the virtues [of the active life] of the just fall into the second rank." [5]

There you have a doctrine universal in the Church, a doctrine which rests on the very word of Christ to Mary that she had chosen the better part. I shall not appeal to the writings of the great mystics, but I shall beg leave to quote here two little books ; a philosopher of your brilliance will perhaps hold them as of small value, but I am bound to them in very special love because they are singularly apt to communicate to the souls of the least of men, of whom I am one, the pure sap of Christian spirituality. These books are *De adhærendo Deo*, attributed to Albertus Magnus, and *La Doctrine Spirituelle* of Père Lallemant. Here are both of them, stuffed into my pocket along with Claudel's *Grandes Odes* and a *Guide for Gardeners*. Read what Master Albert says.

PHILONOUS (*reading*). " Let him who wishes to be raised to perfection be withdrawn entirely within himself : there, let him hold no other object in the eyes of his mind save Jesus Christ, covered with wounds ; and thus let him apply himself carefully and with all his strength to penetrate by Him, into Him : by Him Man, into Him God—by the wounds of the Humanity to the very inmost essence of His Divinity, . . . For in that is the goal of all spiritual exercises, to be borne towards the Lord our God, and to find rest in Him within oneself, by a most pure act of the intellect and a most fervent movement of the will, without the distraction of sensible images."

THEONAS. I read likewise in Père Lallemant : " Without contemplation a man will never advance far in virtue and never be well suited to bring others to advance therein. He will never entirely emerge from his weaknesses and his imperfection. He will always remain bound to the earth and will never be elevated much above the feelings of human nature. Never will he be able to render to God a perfect service. But *with* contemplation a man will do more, both for himself and for others, in a month than without it he would do in ten years."

PHILONOUS. So according to you all the saints have been contemplatives and mystics ?

THEONAS. The best theologians say so : provided, that is, that by these words—understood in their most formal sense—one means the state, with degrees and modalities beyond number, of those who in St. Thomas's language live habitually under the rule of the gifts of the Holy Ghost—particularly the gift of Wisdom.

PHILONOUS. That is surely a long way from Aristotle ?

THEONAS. Not so far as you think. All the principles set forth by the Philosopher as to the primacy of contemplation, remain, provided that they are understood of contemplation as practised by the Christian—by the man, that is, made partaker of the divinity by grace. Grace—being a kind of new nature which super-elevates man in his very being and constitutes him a superman by birth (*ex Deo nati sunt*)—requires that man should have higher operations, for action follows essence, one acts as one *is*.

PHILONOUS. What, then, has become of your intellectualism?

THEONAS. There is a mistake to be avoided on the intellectualism of St. Thomas. He proclaims unceasingly the superiority of the intellect over the will, considered according to the absolute hierarchy of the faculties : and he maintains the pure sovereignty of the intellect in the order of speculative knowledge. But, on the other hand, he maintains, that it is by the will that man is good or bad, using the words " good " and " bad " absolutely and without qualification : he makes judgment depend, in the order of practical and prudential activity, on the appetitive faculties—the faculties, that is, of the will— and upon their rectification : and above all, he most definitely affirms the pre-eminence, considered according to the conditions of this world, of love in human life. He teaches that in heaven, thanks to the light of glory, which will render it capable of direct knowledge of God, the intellect will enjoy its primacy : for it is by the intellect that we shall hold our beatitude, possessing God by the vision of His essence ; but equally clearly he teaches that here below, while it is better to know inferior things than to love them, and although man never loves save what he knows in some manner, yet it is better to love God than to know Him : because love draws us to the thing that we love as it is in itself, according to *its* mode of existing, whereas knowledge renders the thing that we know present in us according to the mode and the capacity of our mind.

Hence it follows that the most elevated knowledge that a man can acquire of God here below—the " quasi-experimental " knowledge of contemplation—is brought to being in the intellect only by charity, which renders us like in nature to God : so that supernatural wisdom, for all that it remains a quality inhering in and perfecting the intelligence itself, yet springs from the affective or " mystical " order.

Christian contemplation then, is distinguished from philosophic contemplation by the three following characteristics :

(*a*) Instead of having for sole end the perfection of him who contemplates, it exists for love of Him Who is contemplated ;

(*b*) It does not stop short in the intellect as in its term, but it passes into the will by love ;

(*c*) It is not opposed to action in such a way as to exclude it, but rather it permits action to overflow from its own super-abundance. For the activity which proceeds from the super-abundance of contemplation befits the sons of a God who not only in Himself enjoys His eternal perfection, but has freely and of His own good pleasure produced works *ad extra*, and sent His Word to accomplish among us the work of redemption.

Such action, then—which is added to contemplation without diminishing it, " by way of addition," says St.

Thomas, " not by way of subtraction "—is proper to the most perfect life, more divine than human, the life that Christ led upon earth ; for this was always the contemplative life, yet from its super-abundance flowed continuously into external activity. *Otium sanctum quærit caritas veritatis, negotium justum suscipit necessitas caritatis.*

Obviously, true contemplation has nothing in common with Quietist pseudo-mysticism. See, also, how Christianity, taking over Greek thought, transfigures and enlarges it, resolving the antinomies that it left unsolved. Wisdom was for Aristotle the aristocratic privilege of the few, because the delight proper to it was the most elevated point of reason and the rarest joy of nature ; Christian wisdom, crying out in the places where men gather, calls to itself all souls, because the delight proper to it is the fruit of grace and of charity and is gathered upon the cross : and the cross no man is without.

The Superman of Aristotle contemplated for himself, and it would have been absurd to imagine a friendship between him and Jupiter ; the Christian Superman, united to God by the participation of charity, and to other men by the communion of saints, cannot make an act of love without the whole balance of both worlds being thereby strengthened. Aristotle said of the solitary that he must be either a beast or a god. For the ancients, solitude and the life of the City were in irreducible opposition. But for us, in the phrase of Père Clérissac, a great religious whose memory I venerate,[6] the Church is at once Thebaïd and city, and the soul there enjoys solitude, *instrumentum congruum contemplationis*, without ceasing to be bound to the mystical body of which it is truly part. It may be said that the unending strife

39

between intellect and love, which divides men with such bitterness and which the modern world has so wildly intensified, is only brought to peace in the light of Christian contemplation.

PHILONOUS. Remember that Auguste Comte did very strongly feel the importance of this strife and the necessity of a reconciliation on higher ground. In his *Politique Positive*, he deplored, if I remember rightly, " the long modern revolt of the mind against the heart."

THEONAS. Littré asserts that Comte was at that time stricken with mental alienation. But Littré thereby shows the narrowness of his own brain. Comte was no more mad at that time than at any other. Ever after his famous " cerebral episode " of 1826, his powerful intellect continually sailed above the abyss of madness, a madness always threatening, yet dominated by force of will.

PHILONOUS. Have you read his curious correspondence with his disciple Dr. Audiffrent ? " In the first part of my career," he wrote in 1851, " I had to construct faith, founded on demonstration, its only modern basis. But in the second—begun six years ago under the sacred impulse given to me which I am doing my uttermost to prolong—I must systematise love."

THEONAS. In spite of this very excellent systematisation, the religion of Humanity never has succeeded, and never will succeed, in harmonising intellect and love : for it oppresses the intellect, while of love it gives no more than a maleficent parody. We do not love one another—I mean with an effective and truly disinterested love—save in God, the first loved. Is not charity a single and indivisible supernatural love of God and of our neighbour ? *Ubi caritas et amor, Deus ibi est.*

Take my word for it, Christian wisdom alone brings the solution. In the absolute order of metaphysical dignity, there is not among human things anything better than the Intellect ; but Charity is better than the best of human things. Here below it is of greater value than the intellect : nothing else is. The true reign of the heart demands the union of the soul with what is better than reason—what Aristotle calls the *Principle* of reason ; and it is, therefore, absolutely inseparable from the reign of truth.

CHRISTIAN HUMANISM

CHRISTIAN HUMANISM

As we made our way back through the white-walled cell which served Theonas for oratory and library, Philonous paused.

" Stop," he cried, " I see on your table Paul Cazin's book. I am curious to know what a hermit can possibly think of *L'Humaniste à la guerre.*"

" He thinks," replied Theonas, " that the author of that work will rank, after a few more books of the same quality, among the masters of our language . . ."

PHILONOUS. And is that all he thinks ?

THEONAS. By no means. I shall speak more clearly. I love *L'Humaniste à la guerre,* because I see shining in it the spiritual perfection of measure and number ; because it recreates the classic combination of strength and charm while yet it has all the purity of the age of La Fontaine ; because with its prudent subtlety, its wise irony, its emotion deep and delicately toned yet never overmastering art, it is a very rare weaving together of Greek and French virtues. But I love it also because along with the savour of classical antiquity, there are mingled ever and again echoes of the sacred chant, and because it bears upon it the promise of a Christian humanism made new.

PHILONOUS. So you do not agree with Bremond that humanism is by nature pagan ?

THEONAS. Assuredly no : though it tends towards paganism in any soul whose noblest energies are ever so little wearied.

PHILONOUS. That needs explanation.

THEONAS. I shall try to explain it further. But you must excuse me if I make an occasional allusion—with discretion, I promise you, and solely by way of throwing light upon my philosophy—to the formulas of the theologians.

It is a normal thing and a reasonable thing that there should be a Christian humanism, and I imagine that only Jansenist bitterness or, at the other end of the scale, a strong prejudice against religion, could find the idea repellent. Humanism—at least when it makes no claim to be a system in its own right, but simply stands as a rich development of graciousness and liberality produced by the antique disciplines and by the love of beauty—is simply the flower of properly human life—above all, of the reason and the virtues of the reason : why then should it not be lifted into a harmony, on a higher plane, with the gifts that come from above to make us partakers of the divine life ? For grace perfects nature and does not destroy it : original sin did not, as Luther and Jansenius thought, bring a radical corruption into our nature and its faculties. Heresy would have it that we had become bad to the very marrow of our bones, and that in consequence philosophy and all the liberal arts—since they flower from a soil essentially corrupt—could be nothing but evil. The Church, on the contrary, teaches that the works of nature and reason are good in themselves : she

46

condemns those who assert that all the actions of the pagans, all the virtues of their philosophers, were but resplendent sins or vices.

Yet though we are not radically corrupt in our very being, we are wounded in our natural activity—like the poor wretch whom Our Lord picked up on the road to Jericho and placed to be cared for in the hostelry of the Church until Himself should return. The Greeks were of all people the most likely to give rise to the illusion of *pure nature*. The degree of human perfection and human wisdom which they were able to attain, thanks to exceptional conditions, for a moment only, and only in the domain of intellectual speculation and the arts, is the measure of perfect humanism : its ruins, the very memory of its achievement, are of themselves most powerful to enchant us. So that it could not again be equalled— certainly it could not be surpassed—save by the effort of a humanity placed in the state, and using all the means, of *redeemed nature*. In fact, if the word " humanism " is to be understood in all its plenitude, then the world knew in the age of St. Bernard and the age of St. Thomas, the joy of a Christian humanism which certainly had its shadows but which shone—closer to our hearts than the humanism of the Greeks—with the supernatural radiance of the divine virtues. It is *that* humanism whose last fires cast the glow of their loveliness in the work of Dante.

Yet few things could be more difficult to maintain in their integrity than Christian humanism, precisely because while it is a divine achievement, it is a human achievement too. Such an achievement is not beyond measure difficult, at least for the few, in the realm of the speculative intelligence which, according to theologians

like Cajetan, was not *wounded* in itself by original sin :
though, as far as its actual state goes, it might almost as
well have been, for it is pitifully weakened and darkened
and suffers hindrance in countless ways by reason of the
disorders of our other powers. But in the realm of the
moral life, on the concrete plane of human conduct,
nature is only too liable—in the very ages in which it
attains among men to a happy plenitude of vigour and
beauty—to fall away from the rigidly pure order of
Charity, love that is of the Creator, to fall under the
order, alas so much easier, of love of the created. Thus
it happened that humanism became in the sixteenth
century a thing that could in no wise be called Christian.
Beautiful as are the forms in which it took so vivid a
delight, yet in it Humanity fell—as the angels fell :
humanity " discovered humanity," as Höffding says :
that is to say, it began to seek in itself its supreme interest,
and seeing itself naked, it was not ashamed as once
in the Garden, but seized with admiration of what it
saw. . . .

The century that followed, set about repairing the
damage. To-day I shall not go into the question of how
far it succeeded. But I should like to remind you of the
curious experiment, by which certain minds, at the end
of the sixteenth century and the beginning of the seventeenth, essayed to make a harmony of the Christian faith
and a kind of neo-Stoic Humanism. They were grave
and reverend personages, Catholics and foes of mysticism :
Guillaume du Vair with his *Sainte Philosophie*, published in
1588 if my memory serves, is their most curious repre-
sentative. But as this Christian Stoicism sought man's
perfection in reason alone, while its tendency was to

confine the Christian energies within the narrow field of the moral virtue of religion—which concerns only the duties of worship—it could not remain really Christian. In fact, it paved the way for the introduction of naturalism into French thought. From this point of view—as M. Strowski has clearly shown—the work of Montaigne (to say nothing of Maître Pierre Charron !) bears witness to the trend of thought of a humanism which was ceasing to be Christian and which, for its punishment, sank down into that cultureless and inartistic thing, moral laicism.

Anyhow, our *Humaniste* is all thronged about with Stoic maxims : " One must be valiant," his spiritual grandparent Montaigne had written, " for oneself and for the advantage that lies in having one's courage lodged in a strong ground and assured against the assaults of fortune." With which compare what Paul Cazin says on his own account : " I have sworn to live as a valiant man and to make necessity my tributary." In the worst situations he is interested not in things, but in his soul. And where does he propose to have converse with his soul ? Not in the interior cell of the mystics, but in that back-shop where Montaigne had converse with his, and among other things kept his library. Listen to him and note the enchantment into which he is cast by the finest things of human wisdom. Notice the use that he makes of the precept to discern, " what depends on us and what does not," and how he believes that " the prayer of the sage is but the supreme exaltation of his will." This Humanist is a first-rate Stoic. And what a moralist ! He has moralising in the blood, like a disease. Certainly—and for this we must be grateful—he brings us forth from the dubious mystery of that " interior life " which Maeterlinck would have us substitute for Christian mysticism : but only that he may cast upon the movements of the soul the rational light of an exclusively philosophic moral system. He does not even—like Du Vair, Montaigne and Charron—make profession of the Christian faith ; he declares—at least at the beginning of his book—that he finds in the depths of himself nothing save " a great resignation to necessity and a firm purpose honourably to bear its inevitable blows," and that he is " full of a feeling of God, an entirely human and unmeritorious mingling of charity and hope."

When an old chaplain asks him " If he has preserved the Christian virtues," he " says yes, and runs away as fast as he can. . . ."

And yet . . . there is something in him beyond this purely human moral outlook. He has nothing of the Kantian, bent like a bow and quivering in his virtue : he has no pride : he can smile at himself and his moral system—and yet not fall into despair or cynicism. And, what is a greater thing, his heart is open to the great flood of sorrow and pity which bears away in its ebb the weakness of man's systems. Stoicism teaches that only the opinion that we have of things renders them either good or bad to us ; and that thus, being master of his own judgment, Zeno is master of the world. When Paul Cazin returns from the fields of horror—a horror recreated in his lucid and measured art better than ever it could be in the most unbridled realism—when he comes down from the wood of Ailly, he knows that Stoicism is a lie. " Cursed be the man who curses not war ! " There you have, and how splendidly, a recoil, a revolt, of which your true Stoic would be incapable ; an agony of the soul invaded by the waters. That is no cry of a humanitarian frenzied in his optimism : it is the cry of a man who has seen with his eyes the misery of earth, whose cause and whose purpose only the Passion of Christ could make plain.

I think he would have to admit that it is only for lack of better that he turns for support to the maxims of the Stoics. Not in them was the cordial that sustained him. The man is essentially not doctrinaire. What aids him to grapple with life is *not* his view of life but rather his art, filling his whole soul with its movement and seeking to impose upon it the same deep-seeing regulation and the same purity of line that it imposes upon his work. But he knows deep down within him that that is only a sort of first aid : art is not enough that man may live and die.

The verses of Scripture which at every conjuncture mount to his lips, the prayers, the psalms, the canticles, which mingle in his soul with remembered fragments of the Odyssey—in repeating all these, he tells himself that he is doing no more than recite fine poetry. He knows himself as an artist in words and so distrusts himself. And in this he is not altogether wrong, for he who merely hears the sacred words and does not *do* them is like a man who looks at his own face in a mirror : as St. James says, " For he beheld himself, and went his way, and presently forgot what manner of man he was." Yet the words you listen to and say over to yourself are active and efficacious, and you know it ; they sink deep into man like a dew from heaven. And it cannot be that a man should hear,

51   E 2

as you hear, the poetry of the Holy Ghost in all the
voices of nature unless his soul is attuned to the breath of
that Spirit.

" The ants run over my bare feet as I stretch them out
in the sunlit grass. From the branches of the pear tree
shaken by the wind, insects fall, of every colour. The
peace of God walks in this orchard, in a troop of turquoise
spiders and agate lady-birds . . . *Venite et videte opera
Domini quæ posuit prodigia super terram, auferens bella usque
ad finem terræ.*"

In all movement the important things are the starting
point and the finishing point—the *terminus a quo* and the
terminus ad quem, as we barbarians say. The humanists of
the sixteenth century abandoned Christ for Seneca. Our
humanist of to-day starts from Seneca—to go where
Seneca cannot follow him.

" What is courage ? " he asks. " It is the keeping of a
serene soul and a free mind in the face of danger. And it
does not surprise me that so many souls—feeling themselves to-day stronger than the death they despise,
lovelier than this wretched body that slobbers with fear
and chatters its teeth, desire to live a life of the spirit and
begin once more to believe in their immortality."

It is thus that humanism begins to turn its face
towards loftier summits. Its task is to climb again in
blood and filth the flowery slope that Erasmus and
Montaigne descended so long ago.

" I went off to a distant sap, solitary as the sparrow of
the Psalm or the owl in his resting place. My heart is
hot within me and my meditation sets me on fire. Sorrow
and joy—Lord show me my destiny. Tell me what is the
number of my days that I may know what remains to me

Thou hast measured my time and my being is as nothing before Thee. Truly all that lives in the world is but vanity : man passes like an image that fades. But Thou, Thou art my expectation, O Lord. Thou art the hope of those who have no other hope. Man would hold it for dishonour thus to be loved last of all, for want of other. But it is Thy eternal glory and the mark of Thy greatness to receive hearts abandoned and the poor remains of vanity.

" Hear the voice of my supplication. Let me not speak without reply. Why art Thou silent ? My reason drives me to Thee and Thou dost cast it back. I seek in Thee the understanding of my being. Thou dost place canticles in my mouth. Illuminate my darkness. Why dost Thou hide Thyself ?

" The soul of man calls upon Thy infiniteness. It is too little to contain it, it breaks under the weight of divinity. *Remitte mihi ut refrigerer priusquam abeam et amplius non ero . . .*"

At the end of the book our Humanist, " dreaming and praying," addresses himself in two parallel prayers to Zeus and to God the Father, yet one cannot but feel that the first prayer is no more than a poetic dream, the dream of the Stoic who is passing, and that the second alone is prayer, the prayer proper to the Christian who will remain.

What constitutes for me the incomparable charm of Cazin's book is this : that it is the totally sincere witness of that movement of flight, of passage, that divine bypath by which the soul, still uncertain, goes towards Him Whom it seeks, and Whom it would not seek if it had not found Him."

PHILONOUS. Do you know whether your Humanist *has* found Him ?

THEONAS. Solitaries, my friend, know many things ; but one is not bound to say all one knows.

THE THEORY OF SUCCESS

THE THEORY OF SUCCESS

WHEN we had returned to Paris, Philonous drew a deep sigh and said : " I have a great esteem for your hermit, and I grant that his intellectual discipline is not without value. It may even be that fundamentally he is right, in spite of his old-fashioned philosophising. But it is well for him that he remains in his solitude ; his ideas are outside life as it is lived now : neither he nor his ideas could possibly succeed. In his presence I felt myself growing unreal as if in some icy waste a shade called up the past before my eyes. Now that we are back in the street, I begin to be myself again. How sweet is the savour of the dear old buses, the evening papers, the cinemas, the airmen, the underground tickets, the progress of science, the Dadaïst reviews, the trade-union posters : they give me back that feeling of the concrete which is, in the phrase of William James, the most venerable reality, object of the most venerable knowledge. For all this newness we must have a new philosophy as well, a philosophy that conforms to the present moment. To succeed, a thing must be *actual*, up to the minute."

" The point is," I replied, " that there are two ways of being actual. What is by its very essence in *time*, is actual only by, and for, the instant. Such, for example, is the ' concrete ' that seems to have such charms for you : it is actual—of the moment—only because it can suffer change. But that which is above time is actual without suffering change. ' God,' someone has said, ' loves the ancient, but not the old.' We are attached, not to the past as such, to that which is past : but to the eternal substance known to time past, to that which does not pass.

" Take the Church. As Benson noted so finely, many good souls take offence at the insolent immutability of its doctrine and its sacramental life, which seems to them a challenge to progress ! And the same good souls are scandalised by the flexibility with which it has met the changing circumstances of its historic development—which seems to them a falling short of the absolute ! The truth is that it is actual, above change, in so far as it is divine ; and that it is actual, *in* change, in so far as it is human. Thus the mountains grow old, but the Church is ancient and never grows old.

" I would say, Philonous, that in principle at any rate, it is the same for the intellect and for wisdom. *Intellectus supra tempus.* The philosophy that is not ancient is very soon old. If a philosophy belongs to the present moment *by its substance and its principles*, surely you must see that its very newness (not being a newness of growth or of achievement, but only a matter of being newly born in time), is a sign that it is inferior to the intellect in that it is subject to the law of matter : for time is a measure of matter's changing. It is true, of course, that philosophy is a human thing : it is in time by the subject wherein it resides—in the philosopher, that is. It must, then, be of the present moment *by its application to the real and by the use made of it*. If it is not, you are right in saying that it will have no hold upon men. The decadent scholastics

of the sixteenth and seventeenth centuries, failed gravely
to fulfil their duty of *temporal actuality* in the use of their
wisdom—having as a matter of fact failed, most of them
at any rate, to grasp the *eternal actuality* of that wisdom as
it is in itself. The Thomists of to-day have no intention
of repeating that failure. Yet their task has grown
singularly difficult in a world whose whole mind is set
upon a science immediately practical in its bearing,
aiming at an exhaustive cataloguing of phenomena and
the individual—and binding the mind in servitude to the
flux of time."

" So you do see that the doctrines of your friend
Theonas have no chance of success. You admit yourself
that they have against them one of the strongest tendencies
of our time."

" As far as that goes, they have against them something
more—namely one of the strongest tendencies of human
nature itself. You will agree that man, by the very fact
that he is a rational animal—the most perfect of animals
and the least perfect of spirits—is a being in whom the
intellect exercises its primacy only with difficulty and
with many an eclipse ; and that an all too natural slope
leads him to search for easy ideas, to economise thought,
to judge according to what he wants and not according
to what is—in short to cripple the intellectual life within
him. Now Thomism is difficult and makes singularly
strong demands in the matter of intellectuality. Think
for a moment of the strange accidents, utterly unrelated
to pure intellect, which may lead to the success of a
doctrine with the public. As to these accidents, by the
way, we owe a good deal of gratitude to the historic
materialism of Georges Sorel, which has shed much

useful light upon them. Anyhow, they make it very extraordinary that a system of thought only too precisely qualified by the word *angelic*, should be having such success among men."

" Very well : you grant all I ask, and more ! "

" I grant you nothing at all. We have not only to consider what you must allow me to call in philosophic jargon, *material* causality, that is, in the present instance, the dispositions of the human subject. *Formal* causality —I mean the value of the ideas themselves and the virtue of the intellect—is, in spite of all, a much more important factor. For example, if Cartesianism triumphed at the end of the seventeenth century, it was not solely because it fitted the ideological needs of a new class and of *honnêtes gens* : it was also because it made use of a certain *truth*—the truth of the physico-mathematical science of nature—though misdirected, pressed into its service, and imprisoned in an erroneous system. In reality, the least germ truly intellectual is, in itself, more efficacious than all the material ' constellations of factors.' It is a thing infinitely little, but ultimately irresistible. From this point of view, I would even say that the less chance of success a doctrine has, because it is too strong intellectually for the human subject, the more reasonable it is to hope that one day it will triumph : for intelligence fights on its side, and God loves intelligence."

THE MATHEMATICAL ATTENUATION OF TIME

THE MATHEMATICAL ATTENUATION
OF TIME *

I

YESTERDAY, at the Café de la Rotonde, Philonous was looking blissful. In the company of the poets Taloff and Dessambre † and a scattering of tall Danes and subtle Roumanians, he was having Einstein's little book *On the Special and General Theory of Relativity* [7] explained to him by my friend Rhodanthus. As his eyes lit on me, he called out excitedly :

" These are wonderful days for science ! What joy to be spectator of a revolution in cosmology as vast as that of Copernicus and Galileo, and more profound. I am filled with a feeling of great joy, with a pleasant internal titillation at the thought that the principle of inertia, Newton's law of gravity, even the ether wherein the physicists used to put out their blackest contradictions to pasture—all have gone out of existence along with poor old Euclidian space. And time ! Dear old time, who thought himself our master ! Then suddenly, late in his career—in 1905, to be exact—there came over him a

---

* Since this chapter was cast into its present form, advances and changes in the ruling ideas of physics have continued to follow one another in rapid succession—Einstein's conceptions have evolved and others have come to complete them. But these changes, I think, do not affect the relevance of what I had written, and it seems preferable to keep to the text of the second French edition (1925). In any case, my primary object was to elucidate the philosophical theory of time held by Aristotle and St. Thomas Aquinas.

† Taloff went to Russia some time ago, and has probably been put to death. Dessambre has become a Carthusian.

change of nature, and he woke up one morning to find himself ' relative.' Undoubtedly the revolution that Einstein has worked, will open unimagined perspectives to scientific spiritualism. Already, so suggestive is hyper-space, several worthy authors have embraced the conception that at the death of the body, the soul makes off without ceremony to the fourth dimension. For me, I feel that I must look upon my soul as a body infinitely depthless, moving with the speed of light : and this thought gives me much strength and consolation. But I must not now enlarge upon these thrilling theories. What I delight to see is that it will become more and more difficult for you to set the empty clamours of common-sense against the progress of research and to found a philosophy on its outworn authority. Do you not see that the further science advances, the further it is removed from common-sense ? ' Good sense is a deceiver,' as Lucien Fabre said."

" You must distinguish, my dear friend," I replied, " and first, do not confuse us with Reid and the Scotch School. We do not rest our philosophy on the authority of common sense, regarded as a blind instinct which imposes itself *in fact* upon all men : on the contrary we say that philosophy is based upon evidence ; upon the evidence of the primary facts attested by the senses, and upon the evidence of intelligible first principles, self-evident truths. For there *are* self-evident truths, whatever modern philosophers may say : otherwise there would be no truths at all—since the truths that can be demonstrated, are true only by reason of the principles that cannot be demonstrated, into which in the end they may be resolved : and these latter—the principles that cannot be demonstrated—must either be self-evident truths or else merely gratuitous assertions or convenient assumptions—in other words mere nothings from the point of view of truth. These self-evident truths we call *natural*, because we only need to understand their terms in order to see that they are true. But we must be careful : the word ' natural ' has, in this use, all its metaphysical value, and not simply a descriptive or psychological value. It signifies not only that we are certain that the truths in question are present *de facto* in the majority of human heads : it signifies also that they spring of necessity, *de jure*, from the activity of the human intelligence functioning as such.

" Therefore you must grasp this : philosophy is for us as it were the scientific and unlimitedly progressive development of that metaphysic which is implicitly professed by common-sense—because it rests, as I have just said, on the understanding of first principles naturally evident, and because it attains by way of proof to the certitude naturally deduced from these principles by common-sense. But that does not mean that we think that ' good sense ' suffices that men may advance in the particular sciences or judge the theories of these sciences, or in Descartes' phrase, ' penetrate into the fullest secrets of the most remote sciences.' We are not Cartesians, and we mistrust *clear ideas*. We believe that science is difficult, only to be acquired by an intrinsic elevation, an inflexibly aristocratic ἕξις of the intellect.

" In short, the *natural truths* of common-sense—as for example that the whole is greater than the part—are to us something altogether different from the *easy solutions* of common knowledge—as that the sun moves round the earth—or of a science superficially clear—as that the substance of bodies is extension. These last are probably what the man had in mind who said that good sense is a deceiver ; and it is in this field that scholars are right in refusing to pin their faith—without serious analytical examination—to the so-called intuitions of this same good sense . . . "

"The history of modern mathematics is a case in point," said Rhodanthus, himself a mathematician. "Consider, for example, the theory of functions and the developments that it has undergone ; whoever would have admitted, before Weierstrass, that there could be continuous functions without derivatives, curves without tangents. Yet it must be added that in certain scientists along with this rightful prudence, there is sometimes to be found mingled a kind of malice—index of a mind fundamentally negative, as Comte would have said— which inclines them to the destruction of common-sense itself. There is an immense pleasure to be gained from proving the falsity of what, until Me, everybody held for true ! "

"That is as it may be," went on Philonous, "but you must admit, my poor Hylas,"—he amuses himself some- times by calling me Hylas in memory of Berkeley, and as a back-handed compliment to my Aristotelianism— "You must admit that Einstein may be right against good sense and that in this matter of time, good sense may be in error."

PSEUDO-HYLAS. No. For the notion of time is a primary notion. It is of course true to say with St. Augustine : "What, then, is time ? If no one asks me, I know ; if I

wish to explain it to one who questions me, I know not."
But it is equally true that the spontaneous knowledge
which common-sense has of it, being truly *natural*, cannot
be false.

PHILONOUS. Then in the name of common-sense you
challenge the whole of contemporary science ?

PSEUDO-HYLAS. Again no. For common-sense and
philosophy are concerned with real time—a physical
reality which is the duration of that which changes ;
while Einstein, in fact if not in intention, speaks of something quite different—namely a mathematical entity
which is a variable in an equation and which has nothing
in common with time, except the name. It would be as
erroneous to claim that Einstein's theories force us to
throw into the discard the idea of time held by common-
sense, as to believe that this same idea obliges us to reject
a priori Einstein's theories—at least when these are
restricted to their purely mathematical signification.
We must distinguish carefully the Time of metaphysics,
or more precisely of Natural Philosophy—what Aristotle
called " Physics "—from the Time of those who theorise
upon the principle of relativity.

You must keep a careful eye on modern physics, my
dear Philonous ; it is marvellously rich and potent, but
deceptive likewise ; and for this good reason, that it is
not properly physics at all—the science of sensible nature
itself and of the real causes concerned therein—but rather
the mathematics of sensible *phenomena*. It is an " intermediate science," a science *formally mathematical*, of which
physical data merely furnish the matter. It has not,

therefore, for its proper object, its *formal* object, the things of nature considered in themselves, neither the principles that constitute them nor their causes; it is concerned solely with one aspect of them, its business is only to establish functions between variable magnitudes and to fabricate an abstract network of mathematical relations, applicable as precisely as possible to natural phenomena. Thus it seems to correspond to Auguste Comte's conception of science; and even then it remains true that the " laws " it discovers manifest a certain sort of " cause "—the mathematical formal cause, or the numerical harmony of creation—and in reality the physicist is ever in search of " causes," though he attains them only symbolically. Yet if one seeks the *laws* without being able to know the *causes* in themselves, one is exposed to the risk of taking mere fictions for causes or for real beings—and this must happen whenever, in spite of the firmest resolutions, one yields to the intellect's instinctive attraction to *being* and so proceeds to attach some physical and ontological value to those *entia rationis* which have to be constructed as a support for the language of mathematics.

" The physico-mathematicians of our day, their ideas clarified by three centuries of experience and by the reflections of authors so diverse in their mental direction as Hirn, Poincaré, Duhem, Mach and others, have for the most part a true idea of the scope of their science; but on the other hand, the founders of quantitative physics firmly believed that they would arrive at a true explanation by causes, and so create a philosophy of nature. And incessantly this illusion lies in wait to entrap the expert. In the case we are discussing, Einstein and his disciples are claiming that as physicists and philosophers of nature, they are reacting against the mathematical preoccupation of the mechanics of their predecessors ; and they really believe that the " time " which they discover at the end of their learned mathematical manipulations of the letter " t," is true physical time.

In reality, for three centuries they have been stripping the notions of *movement* and of *time* to the uses of mathematics, and to-day they have completed this attenuation : yet both these notions belong to the physical, not to the mathematical order. Hence, since they continue to attribute to these notions a physical and philosophic value proper to them only in their fullness, there arise the divagations and the mental vertigo which threaten not only the unhappy public which reads the popularisers of science and the airy romancers of philosophy, but often the men of learning themselves, so that it becomes a matter of urgency to set all honest minds on their guard.

RHODANTHUS.   In fact, eminent mathematicians are declaring to-day that non-Euclidian space has by now acquired an existence that can be, and has been, physically proven.   How dazzling were the metaphysical speculations into which M. Langevin—who some years ago introduced the principle of relativity to the Société de Philosophie—plunged his audience at the Collège de France.   An enthusiastic disciple of his told me of this subject of meditation set forth in all seriousness by the Professor : supposing that the capture of Petrograd by Youdenitch—an event which they were then expecting !— had caused a rise in Russian stocks on the New York exchange ; for observers whirled along by a movement whose speed in relation to the earth was *per impossibile* superior to that of light, the succession of these events would be reversed. Then, O beauty of science ! O relativity of our concepts !—the rise in values would take place first and the capture of Petrograd would limp in a bad second. It is true that the supposition itself is impossible—not for logical reasons, but for purely physical reasons, since no speed can be greater than that of light."

PSEUDO-HYLAS. Why not, while we are about it, choose still more thrilling examples ? With the aid of the principle of relativity I can imagine the woman still beautiful—spoken of by the author of the *Connaissance de la déesse*—leaving her newly-married daughter on the wings of a good genius who would bear her into some part of space with a curvature very different from ours, and on her return, ten minutes later, finding herself the great-grand-daughter of her son-in-law.

II

PHILONOUS. Have your joke by all means, but I would like to know if your philosophers have been able to say anything intelligible about time. " The number of movement according to before and after." [8] Long ago Pascal was laughing at that charming definition.

PSEUDO-HYLAS. Yes : because he was thinking only of verbal definitions, and the word " time " does not need to be defined. But the thing itself needs to be, if not strictly defined, at least " set out " explicitly. I shall try, therefore, to answer your question—and so try your patience.

For philosophers—those that is who believe in the reality of time—mathematical time, infinite and void, is not real being at all, but *ens rationis*, having no existence save in the mind. So far, therefore, our philosophers agree, at least verbally, with the new physicists. But real time, being based upon movement, is, like space, inseparable from matter—so that time and space began to exist only with the corporeal world and are limited as it is.

Consider any portion of extended matter. It has parts, placed one after the others, it has spatial *befores* and *afters*. If a thing in motion traverses this portion of extension, its motion, passing through these diverse parts, will likewise have its own *befores* and *afters*—but with this distinction, that they are successive, that is to say, of such sort that one disappears as the other is about to appear.[9] The succession of these *befores* and *afters* of motion is time itself, which is given as soon as there is change ; or, in more exact terms, it is the fugitive element that we extract from things, in order to constitute that object of thought which we call time. " If the heavens ceased to revolve and the potters' wheel still turned," [10] or even if the life of images and sensations still continued in the soul,[11] time would be there—a reality—yet a reality so poor and so deficient in being that it is *present*—posed in actuality above nothingness—by no part of itself, but only by the indivisible term which binds the future to the past, that is to say, by the *instant* which has no duration.[12] In truth it does not manage to take a hold upon the mind as an intelligible nature, it does not attain completion

71

nor perfect itself as the object of a concept, save by the aid of the memory and the operation of the mind ; for the parts that constitute it cannot subsist together save in a memory which numbers them. Thus we have arrived at the famous definition that you started out by asking me to explain and at the same time we see the factor of ideality that it introduces into time. " If there were no minds, there would be no time," said Aristotle.[13]

III

PHILONOUS.   What !   Was Aristotle a Kantian ?

PSEUDO-HYLAS.   St. Thomas explains the scope of this formula, and I urge you to re-read his commentary on the *Physics*.   " Given numbered things," he says, " their number is also given : since number (*numerus numeratus*) [14] is precisely that which is measured or measurable.   But does the existence of things depend upon our mind ?

PHILONOUS.   I used to think so in the days of my master Berkeley.

RHODANTHUS.   But do you think you could persuade any physicist to believe it ?

PSEUDO-HYLAS.   No : the existence of things does not depend upon our mind : therefore their number does not depend upon it either ; it is only the *application* to the measurable object of a unit chosen by us—numeration let us call it—which, being an act of the mind, depends upon our intelligence.   As sensible things can exist even though no sentient being exists, so numerable things and number itself—number being, as I have said, that which is measured or measurable—can exist even though no mind exist capable of numbering them.[15]

PHILONOUS. Except, O Thomist, the Mind of the Creator.

PSEUDO-HYLAS. The Mind of the Creator does not number things after they exist, but causes to exist both the things and their number, since His knowledge is the *cause* of what *is*.

RHODANTHUS. How then do you explain Aristotle's phrase ?

PSEUDO-HYLAS. I think that it is rather a difficulty that he is setting himself—*forte diceret quis* . . .—than a thesis that he is putting out on his own account.

PHILONOUS. Take the " number of movement according to before and after." Does this exist independently of the mind as well as the number of, say, these glasses and saucers ?

PSEUDO-HYLAS. No. For movement has not, like these glasses, fixed being in things : it passes ; and time likewise. As I said a moment ago, it exists only by means of the *instant*, which ever-changing continuously binds a time which is not yet, to a time which no longer is. If the soul did not exist, yet time would—but in an imperfect manner without ever being as it were brought together and seen in its full relation. Time and movement have no complete or perfect being save in the mind ; but time is ideal only in the measure in which it thus achieves consistency, thanks to the numeration that we affect, which orders and holds together its fugitive parts in our mind. The magnitude of the *befores* and *afters* which compose its everflowing continuity, is independent of this numeration ; even though it never underwent the application of our units, yet as a measurable (though not measured) reality, it would remain intrinsically what it is : precisely as a given quantity—say of dress-material— has its length before the tape measure is put upon it.

RHODANTHUS. That is precisely what the friends of Einstein deny when they set about philosophising.

PSEUDO-HYLAS. Because the poor devils, like so many modern thinkers, though they can rightly use the notion of " being " in the ordinary things of daily life, cannot rise to this notion in the exercise of scientific thought. Therefore they cannot distinguish *quantity*—that is the measurable taken ontologically, in itself independent of us—from *quantity*—that is the measurable as related to our material measures ; in other words, they confuse quantity and relation.[16]

PHILONOUS. Frightful accident ! ! Sensational tele-scoping of predicates ! ! !

PSEUDO-HYLAS. But the metaphysician knows that all that exists is determined—that is to say a thing cannot be both indeterminate and existent. Before it comes to be measured by us, that which is measurable must already exist and have its determined quantity. Obviously the numerical statement of the dimensions in space or time must vary according to the units of measurement chosen : but things have absolute dimensions—otherwise they would have no dimensions at all—they would not exist quantitatively. That which exists, even if only in the imperfect mode in which time exists—that is by the *instant*—is intrinsically determined. The moment there is matter, there is movement ; the moment there is movement there is time—regarded as the mere succession of the parts of the movement, as a quantity [17] in itself numerable before it is numbered—regarded, if you like, in its material reality . . .

PHILONOUS. You mean, taken *materialiter*. I can see that this elegant word is bursting to get itself said.

PSEUDO-HYLAS. Very well. Taken *materialiter*, time flows in an absolute manner—neither quickly nor slowly.[18] We must be careful not to attribute to it characteristics which issue from the measurement of movement by it, and we must be particularly careful not to confuse it with movement, the flowing of a fluid, the passage through space of a runner or any such thing which comes to our imagination when we think of time. It is something *of* movement, it is not movement itself. It is the flux of impermanence in movement, in itself altogether outside the order of speed or slowness. It is the pure and simple magnitude of the constant cessation of being, of the continual disaggregation imposed upon being by change, the relentless progress of the passage towards non-being.

75

The poets have known it better than some of our philosophers.

RHODANTHUS.   The poets *and* the geologists.

PSEUDO-HYLAS.   Like our friend Termier, who happens to be both.

IV

RHODANTHUS.   But I am not yet satisfied.   Precisely because that which exists is determined, it is not enough to say that in itself a magnitude is measurable : ought you not to say that it is also measured ?

PSEUDO-HYLAS.   Measured, certainly ; not of course by us, or by our measures, but by what I may call the ontological measures of nature ; and this means only that before being mathematically brought into relation with a scale chosen by us, a thing is already ontologically determined in its quantity.   It is in this sense that the ancients held that a body is measured not only by our measuring-rods, but by a *mensura intrinseca* which is in it as the accident is in the substance that it informs—to wit, by its own dimensions.[19]

PHILONOUS.   You must be dreaming, my dear fellow. What is this ontological measure that you talk of ? Surely you don't think you are doing your duty by this discussion when you extinguish the clear notion of measure under the ponderous word " ontological." A measure is never anything but a number discovered by an observer using an agreed scale.

76

PSEUDO-HYLAS. Here we are at the very heart of the discussion. The word " measure " has for the philosopher a much wider sense than it has for the physicist.[20] The philosopher says that God's knowledge is the measure of things, and that things are the measure of man's knowledge ; that reason is the rule or proximate measure of human acts ; that *ævum* is the measure of the angelic life, and so on. In all these there is no question of a number discovered by an observer : measure for us is simply that to which a thing is submitted that it may be determined and co-ordinated.[21] This is number when we are discussing magnitude, but number is fixed by the creative knowledge, not by *our* knowledge. That is what I refer to when I say " ontological measure."

PHILONOUS. It seems to me that that is only an extension by way of metaphor of the " measure " of the physicists.

PSEUDO-HYLAS. No, it is a metaphysical concept, transcendent and analogical, which the philosopher abstracts from the typical case of the unit measure of integral number. Note the commonest acceptation of the word " measure "—*that by which the quantity of a thing is known.*[22] The physicist understands this definition *quoad nos*—that by which the dimensions of a thing are known *by us.*[23] The philosopher understands the definition *secundum se :* [24] that by which the quantity of a thing—and not only its quantity but more generally any one of its values or perfections—is known *in itself ;* that is to say is fixed in the intelligible being, is determined and unified. And the measure *he* has in mind places in the things

77

measured a *real* relation, subjects these things to itself, holds them in a real dependence. Taken thus, we might call it *real measure*, in distinction from measure as it is to us, which is only ideal or logical.

PHILONOUS. On all that I reserve my judgment. All I grant is that the worst conflicts often arise from a simple confusing of vocabularies. One and the same formula might be orthodox in the language of a mystic and heretical in the language of a theologian. What would have happened to Angelus Silesius if he had spoken as a metaphysician ?

RHODANTHUS. I am not sure that Angelus Silesius had not certain metaphysical conceptions that were a shade temerarious. What makes it easy to slip is that the fundamental sense of a word, determined in one vocabulary, has its different harmonics in different vocabularies—and the richer its tone, the more numerous these are.

PHILONOUS. Words demand a certain confidence in the understanding of him who listens or him who reads. And this is normal.

RHODANTHUS. And dangerous. But to come back to time and measure : verbal definitions are free. May we not grant our friend Hylas permission to use the word " measure " according to the definition that he has stated.

PHILONOUS. By all means.

PSEUDO-HYLAS. Let us be careful then to preserve the ontological meaning of the word " measure," even when we apply it to an object like magnitude to which physical measure may also be applied. Rhodanthus and I would say that a spatial magnitude—a permanent continuum—is something measurable by our instruments only because it is already ontologically measured or determined.

RHODANTHUS. Which means that we must not only say that time—considered in its material element, in the pure succession of the before and after of motion—is something measurable ; we must also say that time, time as it exists independently of our mind, is something ontologically measured or determined.

PSEUDO-HYLAS. That *is* my idea. I realise that these are notions which our modern gullets find a little difficulty in swallowing. But I hold that they belong to the natural philosophy, solidly based upon reason, of Aristotle and St. Thomas, and not upon the erroneous part of their physics ; and that they are essential to a rationally worked out theory of time. Yes, there is for me an ontological measure—a real or natural measure—which constitutes the formal element of time ; and we must distinguish very clearly—what the older physics was not sufficiently careful to do—this natural measure from the measures that we make—measures which depend upon our conventional units and by means of which we *number* time and give it an existence in our mind as a completed object of thought.

PHILONOUS. If I understand you aright, in order to

establish a philosophical theory of time you distinguish three things :

(1) the measurable thing, in this case quantity as changing ;

(2) real, ontological measure, according to which this thing is, in fact, measured or determined in nature ; and

(3) human or ideal measure, which we use instead of nature's measures—which are not within our reach—in order to determine physical magnitudes from our point of view.

PSEUDO-HYLAS. Correct. I have only to add that the ontological measure of things must itself be divided into *intrinsic* and *extrinsic*.

V

PHILONOUS. And what do you mean by intrinsic measure ?

PSEUDO-HYLAS. In the case of *discrete quantity* (number), intrinsic measure is the unit which serves to constitute its number and which at the same time measures it.[25]

In the case of a *permanent continuum* (extension), I mean by intrinsic measure the actual dimensions which, in-forming a body, determine it in the order of magnitude, and which themselves, like every form, bear within themselves their own determination.[26]

In the case of a *successive continuum* (time), intrinsic measure is the duration itself, the passing and continually renewed existence of the movement, related or capable of being related to one of its own divisions taken as the unit.

The ancients recognised from this point of view a " proper " or " internal " time which is relative to each thing in motion and, so to speak, to the rhythm of its becoming : since it is a movement's duration measured by itself according to the parts that may be distinguished in it ; internal time—as a consequence of this diversity in the scale of the measure—is " as varied as movement and as diverse as the things whose being is in any manner changing and transient." [27]

Considered thus, fifteen or twenty centuries reckoned in the time of a may-fly would equal a month reckoned in the time of man and an imperceptible fraction of a second in the time of the earth ; and the time of the contemplative would be practically motionless by comparison with that of the man of action.

PHILONOUS. In all this you have the disjointed and multiplied duration demanded by the *proper times* of Einstein. It looks like an excellent chance to dress up your scholasticism in the latest fashion.

PSEUDO-HYLAS. The " proper times " of scholasticism are very different from the " proper times " of Einstein ; their multiplicity does not hinder the ontological measurability of the flux of " befores " and " afters " of movements which, varied as they may be, are none the less interdependent and co-ordinated in the unity of the universe.

That is why the schoolmen taught that, as a consequence of the unity of the world, this multiplicity of *proper times* is no more than virtual or material. I remember having read a very remarkable commentary of Cajetan [28] on the subject. If things were each a world apart, each would, in fact, find in itself the measure of its own duration ; but they form a community and are, in consequence, subject to a common measure—extrinsic this time—which as it were prevents their duration from being broken up according to the multiplicity of *proper times*.

RHODANTHUS. To avoid such a breaking-up, would it not be enough that the successive dimension of things— the matter of their *proper times*—is, as we have said, intrinsically determined ?

PSEUDO-HYLAS. That would suffice, certainly, to avoid the dislocation of times and of simultaneities in Einstein's sense.[29] But it would not suffice to submit the variety of durations to a real and positive unity such as is demanded by a world which is one not only materially but also formally.

PHILONOUS. *Omnia in mensura, et numero, et pondere disposuisti.* It is a question of the unity of the universe as a work of art, as a product of the divine industry. That, I suppose is why you do not rest content with intrinsic ontological measure, but must introduce also the extrinsic.

PSEUDO-HYLAS. Yes : and if you get rid of this notion, you might, it seems to me, evade, but you could not solve, the problem of the unity of time. The thought of St. Thomas, at any rate, is quite clear : given that things form part of the universe, they do not find in themselves the measure of their continued existence, that is of their duration.

There must then, of necessity, be a real measure which effectively numbers all the durations of this world, a time that may be called " extrinsic " because it is applied from without to all individual movements and individual durations—whether it be itself the internal time of a *mobile determinatum*, as the early scholastics held, or of the universe in its entirety as we hold to-day. In short, because the world is one, time is one : not only as to a common measure possible in the abstract, but also as to the real measure of the diverse fluxes of duration. That is why St. Thomas always holds very firmly that, given any movement whatever, time also must be given, but that all the same there is in fact, here below, but one sole time, that of the first movement.[30]

VI

PHILONOUS. Is not this doctrine bound up with the theory of the first heaven and all that astronomy which is now on the scrap heap ?

PSEUDO-HYLAS. That is a mere confusion of mind on your part. The unity of time is bound up, not with the first heaven of Hipparchus and Ptolemy, but with the unity of the world. Surely you know that St. Thomas likewise admitted one single measure of duration for the *angelic* world. In their case there was no question of spheres and their circulation in the heavens. But because pure spirits form a community, and because their duration must, in consequence, have a common measure, and because in all orders of being the measure is whatever is most simple,[31] it is the substantial duration of the highest of the angels and the succession of his thoughts which measure the *ævum* and the discontinuous time of all the others [32] . . . The first heaven was, primarily, for these earlier philosophers, a convenient foundation provided by the astronomers, whereon to base the one single time *demanded* by philosophy ; and you know that in a general way, the great errors of their physics are due to the very influence exercised by metaphysical truths upon the science of matter ; a misuse of pure reason insistent upon satisfying itself in the *sensible*, which is not its right atmosphere. We have grown more careful. But it would be absurd to reject along with the astronomical error the philosophical truth of quite a different order which did no more than make use of it and did not in any way depend upon or arise from it.

Annexing—and sacrificing—physics to metaphysics, they were only too willing to take our sensible measures as the *translation* or projection of the ontological measures of nature. Our scientists of the present day, on the other hand, can make nothing of what has not been attained by means of their instruments—the ontological measures of nature and the absolute existence in things of measurable reality (quantity, dimensions).[33] In reality our measures, being essentially relative, do not permit us to seize, in itself and in its own divisions, the time of the universe, the extrinsic ontological measure of all individual durations ; we are forced to rest content with practical equivalents, choosing for example—as has been done up to the present—a universal mode of reckoning which is

no more than the most regular which is possible to us ;
but there is no earthly reason, if science finds it useful,
why we should not adopt in preference the spatio-
temporal method of reckoning in four dimensions used
by the theory of relativity. In either case it is a mere
method of reckoning, and does not prevent things from
remaining what they are, nor does it in any way change
the existence of universal time.

RHODANTHUS. Here you touch upon a mistake too
often made in scientific ideology, the mistake of identifying
things with the manner in which they fall within our
mathematical determinations, or within the measure of
our senses or our instruments. That, for instance, is why
Descartes regarded movement as "reciprocal". He
argued : it is a matter of indifference whether I say that
I go towards the goal or the goal comes towards me,
because in either case the variation in the relations of
distance is exactly the same. And, in fact, for mathematicians there is nothing to be considered in movement
save such variation in relation to axes of co-ordinates
arbitrarily chosen. The very reality of movement, which
concerns physics or natural philosophy and not the
science of abstract quantity, altogether escapes mathematics as such. Nothing could be truer than the
" principle of relativity " held since Galileo by the older
mechanics—as, for instance, when it is said that : " Two
observers travelling with a rectilinear and uniform movement can only perceive their movement relative to each
other " : or again that : " By no mechanical experiment
can one render evident the rectilinear and uniform movement of a system, if such experiments are made within

the system." These phrases signify that absolute move-ment—whether or not it exists—is at any rate not dis-cernible by our science. But I am afraid that for a great number of scientists they signify that no absolute move-ment exists at all. Yet that is really a different question —a question for natural philosophy and not for experi-mental physics. I think I perceive a similar confusion in Einstein's speculations on simultaneity, which he sets out to define without ever considering it in itself and as a concept, but always and solely in the means we have of being aware of it.

PSEUDO-HYLAS. The relativity of time taught by Einstein thus concerns the art of forming a mathematical systematisation of the sensible measurements that we make of the universe ; but regarded as a philosophic doctrine of the real, it is literally nonsense, it has no meaning at all.

PHILONOUS. Yet if all observable movements—and particularly the first movement as your Aristotle says, the movement of the earth—became say, twice as slow, our time would give place to another time, and we should have no means of perceiving it.

PSEUDO-HYLAS. Quite so. And it would be the same with extension in space, if all dimensions became at once and in the same proportions greater or smaller. But what does that prove ? We should not perceive the change ; yet it would remain true that there had been a change, and that a section of the new-fashioned time would really be equal—without our knowing it—to such and such a different section of *our* time, thus ideally prolonged. Our time might cease to exist, some other time might exist after it, just as another time might co-exist with it in a world separated from ours : each of these different times measures in its own manner a succession of *before* and *after* whose magnitude is something ontologically determined in itself and hence absolute—with the result that the diverse measurable durations, considered in themselves, maintain an unvarying relation one to the other. Your remark—which in any case is not particularly novel —has nothing to do with Einstein's theories.

For Einstein, if the unit of measure of the time of one system varies from the unit of measure of the time of another, the reason is that the flux of the instant, the very flowing-by of successive duration, is such that the relation between the diverse measurable durations varies from one system to another, according to the relative speed of these systems. From this it follows that what is *present* in the duration of one, if it is an event distant in space, is *more or less past*, or *more or less future* in the duration of the other ; two events which are simultaneous in the time of one system are thus successive in the time of the other. You remember the example, by now classic, of the footboard of a train passing at full speed by the platform of a railway station ? On the train are two observers, A and B, separated from each other by a certain distance ; on the platform of the station are two other observers, A^1 and B^1 separated from each other by the same distance. When the train passes, A passes before A^1 at the same instant that B passes before B^1—by the station time !— but by train time A^1 does not pass before A at the same instant that B^1 passes before B.

This conception of time, if it were given a truly physical

or philosophic signification, would lead to the wildest metaphysics, to heaven knows what ultra-Leibnitzian universe, at once idealist and pluralist, in which not only would each thing in motion be a world apart in relation to all other things in motion, and everything disjointed from everything else, but there would reign—in opposition to the theory of relativity as a scientific theory—a perfect philosophic relativism in which the category *quantity* would be perpetually identified with the category *relation*.

VII

PHILONOUS. I shall now overthrow you, my poor friend, with your own arms. Did you not admit a little while back that for the earlier philosophers, if there were several distinct universes each with its first heaven, there would be several distinct times?

PSEUDO-HYLAS. That is the constant teaching of Aristotle and St. Thomas.[34]

PHILONOUS. Very well ; the *proper times* of Einstein are no more objectionable. Withdraw your big words—idealism, relativism, and other such mouthings—and say quite simply that from your point of view the revolution worked by Einstein consisted, in so far as it concerns time, in breaking up the unity of the world as it used to be, and in making of each system, as you have just said, a sort of separate universe. That I grant you : but *you* must grant *me* that one does not thereby introduce any absurdity into the theory of time ; it is the very same hypothesis that the ancients held, when they said that different worlds would have heterogenous times.

PSEUDO-HYLAS. I grant you nothing. What did the plurality of these times mean to our philosophers? That in each of the worlds in question, the ontological measure of all the particular durations—the number of the *befores* and *afters* of the movement of the first heaven, as the supreme Intelligence knows it—would be different. Thus what is *formal* in time would vary from one world to another, and one would have a multiplicity of times without any real common measure—as many times as worlds.

But when we come to what is material, though the real flux of the parts of the movement would be different from one world to the other, yet the measurable dimensions—considered in abstraction—of these different fluxes, would remain absolutes and comparable ; so that there would then be real times ' numerically multiple ' (one per world) —yet all the same the mind could still imagine an ideal time ' specifically ' one.[35] And why ? Because, if among these multiple worlds there is no one common real time, yet there must be among their events absolute simultaneities.

PHILONOUS. Here we are back again at your beloved simultaneity.

PSEUDO-HYLAS. Because it is at the heart of the problem.

PHILONOUS. Ah ! *I* should say rather that here the notion of simultaneity loses all meaning.

PSEUDO-HYLAS. Try to grasp that the notion of simultaneity, like the notion of duration, transcends the notion of time ; they are abstracted from it, of course, as concepts formed by our mind since we always begin with what is perceptible by the senses ; but in themselves, and as the objects represented by those concepts, they belong to a totally different order, much higher and vaster ; they are of the metaphysical order. Time is the succession of *befores* and *afters* of movement in that which changes ; neither simultaneity nor duration have in themselves any connection with succession or change at all. Duration may be identified with the very existence of things—it is their existence simply considered as not ceasing, not destroyed.[36] The idea of duration is a transcendental idea, and analogous, like that of being itself : therefore it may be applied to the eternity of God, and to the *ævum* or discontinuous time of the angels, as well as to our continuous time, which measures the duration of mutable substances, but is itself only the duration—that is the being, unceasingly renewed—of motion.[37]

PHILONOUS. And what follows from that ?

PSEUDO-HYLAS. It follows from that that simultaneity, like duration, is to be defined in terms of *being*, and hence in a manner totally independent of our sensible measurements and our evaluation of time.

PHILONOUS. I should be interested to know such a definition.

PSEUDO-HYLAS. Then follow this chain of reasoning.

Suppose an event happening in any particular duration —say the thought that came into the mind of Nathanael under the fig tree ; this event occupies a very small section of the time of Nathanael, which we can treat for practical purposes as an instant—that is, as an indivisible component of duration. At the very instant thus marked by this thought in the duration of Nathanael, Christ, passing by, looks upon him. Everyone will agree that these two events are simultaneous.

RHODANTHUS. The relativists, too, like everyone else ; it is what they call in their jargon a *spatio-temporal coincidence*. The two events under consideration take place in one same spot ; their simultaneity is absolute.

PSEUDO-HYLAS. Now let us abstract the intelligible content of this example. At the instant marked in Nathanael's time by an event which takes place in that time. . . .

PHILONOUS. And a particular point of space, don't forget that proviso.

PSEUDO-HYLAS. Put that in too, if it pleases you. At the instant thus marked in Nathanael's time, another event takes place in the time of Him Who looks on him. We have two durations, two events, and an instant marked in one of these durations. That is all that we need that we may define simultaneity. We may say that two things are simultaneous if, at an instant fixed in the duration proper to a being, one of these things is given in that duration and the other is also given, whether in that duration or some other.

Don't you see that at the instant marked by my watch in the duration of the way, the two events A and B produced on that way—whether they arise in the duration of the way or that of the train, and no matter what may be their distance one from the other—either take place or do not take place, exist or do not exist ? Existence or non-existence, either way the thing is absolute. It would need a very poverty-stricken philosophy to imagine that distance makes any difference.

RHODANTHUS. The trouble, as we have said, arises from a confusion between simultaneity itself and the sensible standard by which we are aware of it. We cannot appreciate simultaneity at a great distance without introducing certain conventions—for example— if it will help our physics to save its face, the fundamental conventions of the theory of relativity. But simultaneity itself is totally independent of these conventions. *To know if* two events one at Pekin and the other at Paris have been simultaneous, we must first have regulated the clocks of observers in Paris and Pekin according to certain principles. But the definition of simultaneity—*what* it *is*—does not pre-suppose any preliminary establishment of some such relation. Granted that we shall never have a certain criterion of the absolute simultaneousness of two events distant one from the other in space ; yet that proves nothing against the existence of absolute simultaneousness.

PSEUDO-HYLAS. Let us go back to the example we considered a moment ago. *Cum vidi te sub ficu.* . . . Between the look with which Our Lord looked upon

Nathanael and the thought that he read in Nathanael's mind there is absolute simultaneity. So far there is no difficulty. But Christ, in the divine essence, knew intellectually by the Beatific Vision, all creatures and all places whatsoever. Therefore at that same instant fixed in *His* duration *He* must have seen John baptising in the Jordan and Tiberius strolling about Rome. These events, then, were also absolutely simultaneous, for there is no question here of the transmission of some signal which might introduce all the difficulties that we see in the measurement of time : we are concerned with a knowledge that in one act embraces all space.

At this moment, my dear Philonous, you are lighting a cigarette. Your guardian angel sees this event which is happening at a certain instant of your time.

PHILONOUS. I do not believe in angels.

PSEUDO-HYLAS. A sign of weakness of mind. In any case your belief or disbelief in them is of no importance for my argument, which demands not that your guardian-angel should exist, but only that he should be conceivable. Now you grant, I imagine, that the notion of a pure spirit is a conceivable notion ?

PHILONOUS. Go on.

PSEUDO-HYLAS. An angel, then, is looking at you, or at any rate could be looking at you, and at the instant, marked in your time, that you light your cigarette and he sees you as you see yourself—does this pure intelligence see, or does he not see, some event that is happening at Rome or at Moscow ?

PHILONOUS. He sees it, my dear fellow. He sees your friend Chesterton at Beaconsfield, dictating to his secretary a phrase to the effect that it is miraculous that the sun should rise every morning.

PSEUDO-HYLAS. Very well then : at the Rotonde and at Top Meadow, you have two events absolutely simultaneous. And it would be just the same if Chesterton dwelt in a universe separate from ours, a Chestertonian universe. . . .

PHILONOUS. It would be a jolly place, with Ariel tossing the stars in play.

PSEUDO-HYLAS. Very well then : or even if his duration was in a time other than our time.

PHILONOUS. Between an event in that world and an event in this, you say that there would be simultaneity, although there is no time common to both worlds.

PSEUDO-HYLAS. Yes.

VIII

PHILONOUS. I was nearly taken in by your sophisms. But I can catch you out. You first supposed two worlds each with its own time and by hypothesis these times were different from each other. Are you not now surreptitiously introducing a time common to these two worlds, practically the same thing as absolute time in Newton's sense, time that exists before things, an idea which you affect to treat with the contempt it deserves ? This is how it works : " simultaneous " equals " happening at the same time." But as soon as you think of *at the same time*, you think of a *same time*.

PSEUDO-HYLAS. Words, my dear fellow, merely words. Your argument only shows that to design an analogous notion like that of simultaneity, we make use of a word borrowed from the particular application of the analogy which falls under our senses, a word derived from simultaneity as we perceive it in our time. It is mere poverty of language, no more. But I have already reminded you that simultaneity, like duration, transcends the nature of time itself, and *a fortiori* of this or that time ; and the definition I suggested to you purposely made mention of an instant marked in one only of the durations, in order not to presuppose one same real instant common to both—for this *a priori* would make of both one single duration. There can be simultaneity without common duration or common measure of duration, and that is precisely what my argument showed. Between the two separate universes that we imagine there is no common duration, any more than between our world and the angelic : neither the flux that is measured nor the scale by which it is measured are common to both. Yet there is simultaneity between these two separate times, just as there is simultaneity between the continuous time of matter and the discontinuous time of the angelic operations, between time and *ævum*, finally between both these and the divine eternity, which in its indivisibility co-exists with every moment of created being.[38]

And as the simultaneity between any given thought of

an angel and any given event upon earth is absolute, so also between two events taking place in our one world but at a distance from each other. To talk of the relativity of our realisation of the simultaneous is quite licit : but to talk of the relativity of the simultaneous itself is simply not to know what one is saying.

RHODANTHUS. I think so too. And there is the central absurdity, not of the theory of relativity, which is in itself nought but a pure physico-mathematical construction, but of any philosophy that seeks to find in this theory a view into the fundamental nature of things.

Note, too, that they make *local time* a function of speed, and this would be an unpardonable fallacy in any theory of real time : for clearly the concept of speed necessarily presupposes the concept of time, for speed is measured by time, not time by speed. Time is neither slow nor fast, as our friend Hylas told us a moment ago.

PHILONOUS. Twenty-one pages ago !

RHODANTHUS. That just remark of the earlier philosophers. . . .

PSEUDO-HYLAS. Thinkers do not worry much about contradictions when they remain merely dialectic and are not reborn into mathematics. And from their point of view they are not altogether wrong ; the earth's motion collided, so to speak, with contradictions that Galileo could not resolve—partly perhaps because they were not raised till later !

96

RHODANTHUS. Will you allow me to set before you a little conundrum which seems to me to have a certain piquancy for amateurs of controversy ? It brings to light one of the pleasantest contradictions of the system.

PHILONOUS. From Zeno onwards motion and time have been a mine of sophisms, and the mine is nowhere near worked out. But go on.

RHODANTHUS. You know that in Einstein's theory, if a thing travelled with the speed of light there would be for it no displacement in time. It would, therefore, not grow old, time would be annihilated for it. But is not light itself a thing that travels with the speed of light ? Therefore, for light, time is not. But a thing for which time is not is a thing for which there is no past and no future, no before and no after—a thing, therefore, for which there is no motion. Now if light is motionless, how can it have the greatest speed that can be ?

That is my little argument. In the eyes of scientists it is altogether negligible, but it seems to me not without force against the philosophers of nature who take Einstein's theory for a theory of real time.

IX

PHILONOUS. It may be because we do not fully understand the idea of relativity that we are timorous and find contradictions precisely where, if only we gave ourselves completely to the theory, we should discover the most shining horizons.

PSEUDO-HYLAS. It would be truer to say that the idea of relativity is a potent and fecund idea, but difficult to handle and perilous to the reason. The scholastics made much play with it, with all their *secundum quid ;* but they could distinguish what is proper to things themselves and what belongs merely to our way of conceiving them. Relativity, understood mathematically and so used, is called upon to play a greater and greater part in our physics. But in metaphysics great minds have been led astray by the most commonplace examples of reversal of appearance due to a reversal of point of view— by the realisation, for instance, that the mountain of La Cicada is small and bare if you look at it from Vesuvius, and Vesuvius small and bare if you look at it from La Cicada : honestly there is nothing more profound than that in what Henri Poincaré has to say of the inhabitants of an earth perpetually enfolded in clouds, who might attribute centrifugal force either to the movement of rotation of the earth or to some external field of origin : nor in Einstein's example of a man in a lift moving in the void, infinitely far from our stellar system, who would never discover whether it was the accelerated movement of his lift or the influence of a gravitational field acting upon him that held him to the floor. One might write a curious history of the dream-structures built upon the relative by absolute minds, and of the illusions engendered by the idea of relativity among the philosophers—from Nicolas of Cusa, Giordano Bruno, Leibnitz—to speak only of moderns—up to certain disciples of Einstein.

RHODANTHUS. It must not be forgotten that even from the purely physico-mathematical point of view,

Einstein's theories are still very far from compelling acceptance, in spite of the exact facts—not so numerous, by the way, as is claimed—that they have enabled scientists to predict : for after all, the conclusion of an argument may be true, even though the premises are false. There are eminent physicists who reject them, other eminent physicists who hold that they must at any rate be amended. Pierre Duhem, who was in a position to judge them at their first entry upon the scene, saw in them only a sort of pyrotechnics of the geometrical mind ; and it may well be questioned whether the experiment of Michelson and Morley is not susceptible of a different explanation, even if one chooses to hold as proven the views of Maxwell and Lorentz. And, of course, to be strictly logical, between Fizeau's experiment and the conclusion drawn from it that the earth does not bear its ether with it, there is a considerable gap.

PSEUDO-HYLAS. Those are questions that must be left to competent judges. It is our good fortune to hold a certain conclusion, and one of great importance : modern physics—and still more the new-wrought physics of our own days, which springs from the Newtonian physics as the butterfly from the crysalis—modern physics, then, the physico-mathematical science of nature, does undoubtedly attain the real—precisely in this sense that the standards of measurement found by us in the world, upon which it works, are truly something real, are grounded in the real. But once we emerge from the altogether relational realm of measure, once we try to place it in regard to the absolute realities that every relationship presupposes, particularly in regard to the absolute reality of quantity itself and duration, modern physics is no more than a mathematical symbolism with not a shadow of a claim to represent directly that which is. In fact, it manifests a capacity for generalisation, a rich fertility in discovery : it can stimulate thought to feverish activity. These powers it has, and the less it bothers about pinning down its symbols upon natures and causes really existent in the world, the more marvellously are its powers manifested ; but that obviously means renunciation of contact with the real in everything save the starting points of its experiments and the agreement of its numerical results.[39] If it is possible to use Einstein's principle of relativity without absurdity, it is only because of this : that—whatever Einstein may think— the time they speak of in enunciating the principle has been emptied of all philosophic signification, has become only an algebraic entity, founded certainly in the real, upon sensible measurements taken of the real, but in itself not capable of representation. The same must be said of their " space," " non-Euclidean in the vicinity of astral masses," of " mass " that varies with its speed, of " energy " indiscernible from mass, of " force " indiscernible from acceleration—in fact of all the elements of the new scientific synthesis founded upon the principle of relativity. Thus Einstein's theories, since apart from mathematics they have no hold upon thought, could not possibly furnish us with any kind of figure or idea of the world—save a sort of myth with no other purpose than to offer a support for the imagination at the end of a chain of mathematical reasoning ?

PHILONOUS. But why this divorce between mathematics

and physics ? Should it not be possible to harmonise the mathematical interpretation of phenomena with a conception of the world conformed to the principles of a sound philosophy of nature ?

RHODANTHUS. For that it would need some great philosophical genius first to submit to a complete revision the mighty assemblage of hypotheses and theories that are intertwined in modern physics with facts and laws duly established, and then to build together all truths rightly proven in a phraseology of reasonable coherence.

It would be almost a superhuman task—and certainly the scientists would take no interest in it. For their part they will continue to push ahead, giving no thought to the fallacies and philosophic errors from which the great and age-long enterprise upon which they have embarked may suffer. After all, they would say, *does* it suffer ? And need one settle the question in order to discover and formulate more facts ? Never forget that what in our days is called science obeys the law of art rather than the law of science properly so called : it is less concerned with the mind's conformity to the real and with logical coherence, than with the fabrication of a system of concepts and formulas which will offer the best return in practical applications and the discovery of new facts.

THE MYTH OF PROGRESS

THE MYTH OF PROGRESS

" Man's perfectibility is really indefinite : the progress of this perfectibility, henceforth independent of every power that might wish to arrest it,
has no other term than the duration of this globe whereon nature has cast
us."—CONDORCET.

" Whether man attacks his victim on the boulevard or stabs his prey in
unknown forests, is he not the everlasting man, the most perfect of the
beasts of prey ? "—BAUDELAIRE.

PSEUDO-HYLAS. But why, my dear Philonous, have
you brought me on the way towards the valley of Chev-
reuse ? I suppose you want to pay a visit to our austere
Theonas, though it seemed to me that you and he were
scarcely twin minds.

PHILONOUS. I wish to secure your friend's adhesion to
a plan which may startle the timorous, but which offers
an infallible means of social reconciliation and of order
in progress.

PSEUDO-HYLAS. May one know something of this
magnificent plan ?

PHILONOUS. The principle is quite simple. It has often
been remarked that the communist way of life, to which
so many of our contemporaries aspire, finds its perfect
realisation in the monks, who did not have to wait for
Lenin to abolish individual ownership. . . .

PSEUDO-HYLAS. Their own, my friend, not other

people's. But this is a subtle distinction which we may perhaps for the moment neglect. Is it your idea to invite these contemporaries of ours, the adherents of integral communism, to enter the religious orders in a body ?

PHILONOUS. No, no ! Such a solution would be eminently retrogressive, charged with disastrous consequences for the continuance of the race. My idea is exactly the opposite—that the monks should be formed into professional groups and affiliated to the T.U.C. Theonas could give us very strong help in the enterprise if he would found a union of contemplative hermits, to be known as the U.C.H. This organisation would be the first application of the social remedy of which, with modest pride, I am offering the prescription to thinking minds. Bolshevize Christianity and Christianize Bolshevism. To my way of thinking, every true Liberal must see in this formula of perfect union the most modern and the most complete expression of his sublime ideal.

PSEUDO-HYLAS. Explain further.

PHILONOUS. Since the decline of the authoritarian ideas which the Protestant reformers themselves had inherited from the Middle Ages, the effort of the greatest minds, animated by a wide and fecund liberalism, the effort of such as Jean Bodin, Leibnitz, Lessing, Herder, has always tended towards the achievement of a union among men transcending all dogmatic differences—universal union, or better, universal unity, by man and for man, union in the goodwill of the *subject*, to use your jargon— in contrast with union in the light of the object—of that very problematical object from which Kant has delivered us. At the very highest point of these noble aspirations, it is surely becoming that we should place the fraternal embrace of men—for example Christians and Bolshevists—separated by the widest objective differences, between whom there would thereupon inevitably be set up a tranquillising osmotic current. Thus—in absolute contrast with the older type of unity represented at its highest point by the Catholic Church and claiming to unite men by a truth and for a good which have always, *in fact*, been a sign of contradiction—you have in clear outline the modern concept of the city of God.

PSEUDO-HYLAS. It is true, and the League of Nations may be regarded as a first realisation of the ideal—frail, perhaps, and rather sketchy and tentative, but full of possibilities. The older philosophers on the other hand, thought that only light can be a principle of union, *intellectualia et rationalia omnia congregans, et indestructibilia faciens*, as Dionysius the Areopogite says. . . .

PHILONOUS. Pseudo-Dionysius, you mean.

PSEUDO-HYLAS. If you like. And light is essentially objective—the light of being, which derives, in all degrees of created participation, from the eternal and subsistent light. And all who will not recognise the light are by that very fact outside the unity, since light is at once the principle of peace and the sign of contradiction. To make of many men something truly one, nothing will suffice save the divine light in person who builds them all into the union of His Mystical Body.

You must admit, too, that the humanitarian subjectivism and concentration upon the *ego* which you admire, have yielded some charming fruits of peace this last century and a half, and promise fruit still more charming in the years to come. Yet, to come back to your project, I agree that it denotes a certain practical genius.

PHILONOUS. I think so too. I go further than Auguste Comte. He was really and fundamentally a reactionary, and in his celebrated attempt at an alliance with the " Ignatians," succeeded only in incurring the most pitiful humiliations. In my plan the monks, the most completely typical representatives of tradition and the past, are placed at the head of the movement which is to shape the future ; they will direct it towards its goal as wise and moderate men, whereas the Bolsheviks make the mistake of wishing to hurry things rather faster than is reasonable. Thus, without the shedding of blood, with an ease and smoothness for which history has no precedent, there will be achieved the great transformation to communism, which in any case must inevitably come to be, since it is in the direct line of Progress, and you know as well as I do that the law of Progress nothing may resist.

PSEUDO-HYLAS. What I *do* know in this matter of Progress, is that the very idea of necessary and universal progress is, strictly speaking, not an idea at all. It is not a concept whose purpose is to furnish the intellect with a hold upon the real, and therefore the intellect cannot measure or rectify it. On the contrary it is one of those merely verbal formulas—which are more perfect in their order in proportion as they are more independent of, and remote from, and arbitrarily imposed upon, things. If you would understand their origin, go back to the Cartesian *clear idea*. From the *clear idea* pass on to the *facile idea*—facile in that it allows of the very widest application, and explains the greatest number of things with the least effort—effort of thought particularly. From that you pass easily to the *idea-feeling* which, applied to things without taking account of their distinctive natures and enfolding within its wide sympathy all fields of thought, connotes no more than an affective state or a practical attitude of the thinking subject. And now at last, at a third remove from the *clear idea*, you arrive at what I can only call the *idea-myth* which, emptied of all intelligible content and having no other end save to stimulate in the imagination and the appetite certain well-recognised and pleasurable reactions, dominates despotically the whole field of representation and the individual himself, whom it sets a-quiver the moment it is put before his mind. Thus have come to birth those ideological divinities, those pseudo-ideas wherein the real is altogether swallowed up, which in their totality constitute modern mythology : in their very front rank shines the idea of Progress.

PHILONOUS. You are certainly very difficult to follow— I am not sure that I understand you at all. The idea in question is that the progress of the human race is " as necessary as the growth of trees and plants," as the Abbé Terrasson said in the eighteenth century, and that it " takes place in virtue of a natural law exactly similar to that law by which a man grows from infancy to age " : thus the new is, of necessity and in every field, better than the old. Now for me, this idea would seem to have no need of verification by observed fact : it takes hold of my mind as a thing immediately evident.

PSEUDO-HYLAS. I dare say it does. How otherwise can I explain the strange phenomenon that in spite of all the most catastrophic denials of your principle that life provides, you remain utterly undisturbed in your adoration, contemplating with a conscience at peace the disasters already brought upon the human race by the idolatry of this idea, and, undiscouraged, pinning to the future all the hopes that the present so vigorously denies.

" In truth," said Theonas at this point, for he had joined us some little time before : it was his habit to come forth to meet his guests, and indeed but for his fear of seeming a trifle odd, he would have prostrated himself before them, saluting Christ in them, according to the rule of St. Benedict—" In truth, the dogma of the necessary progress of the human species proceeds from a very simple fact about movement which common-sense cannot help seeing—but a fact falsely interpreted and generalised by metaphysical sloth in obedience to the law of the minimum intellectual effort.

" Consider motion or change from the point of view of what we call *form*—meaning thereby that constituent of things which determines and qualifies them from within. Take, for example, a case in which matter is perfectly dominated by form, such as an organism in its period of growth. Common-sense immediately sees that in that case change is produced in accordance with the law which ordains the less perfect to the more perfect, infancy to the prime of life. Now because, in such a case, we have to consider only what the *form* demands, change proceeds towards the more perfect according to the law of Progress.

" But we have not only the form to consider : there is also the matter—what St. Augustine calls ' pure mutability '—which, since it is in itself absolutely nothing determined—therefore in itself not a thing—becomes this thing or that thing only when it receives a form. Now philosophers tell us that matter has a kind of appetite for form, being itself only potentiality : hence a passive desire, an aspiration of formless passivity towards actual and determined being. But notice : this appetite in matter by no means tends to the more perfect forms to the exclusion of the others. On the contrary, it tends to any and all forms, whatever they may be, provided that they *are* forms and that they confer actuality : it tends to submit itself to the imprint of all aspects of being, to adapt itself to all possible varieties of determination and completion, to achieve the *adæquatio formarum*. This desire— using desire in the sense given above—is never fully satisfied, and ever, in its measurelessness, overflows present possession : for matter cannot at any moment have a form save on the condition of not having all the other forms : and this desire, this eternally wandering appetite, underlies all the ceaseless flux and reflux of universal mutation."

PHILONOUS. You are turning poet, my dear Theonas : you sound as though you were describing, not the appetite of matter, but rather a romantic state of soul.

THEONAS. In truth, the eternal unappeasement of desire is proper to matter, which Plato called *existent non-*

being ; and when Giordano Bruno, Lessing and all the worshippers of becoming make it their boast that they would rather seek than find, aspire than know, desire than possess, in their wish to be for ever unsatisfied, they are merely imposing upon the human creature the law of that which is formless as such, of that which is lower than all. If the human soul does not find rest in any created thing, it is not because it is made for endless movement, but only because it is made to find rest in the Infinite.

But let me resume the thread of my thoughts. Since the appetite of matter is as I have just said, it follows that even in the most perfect forms it still keeps in its very roots the desire for other forms, simply because they are other. In the animated organism it continues to desire the inferior forms of non-living elements, and the corruption of the living being is for it a good, a momentary satisfaction of this desire for some form other than that which at the moment it has. Hence if we consider the appetite of matter, change, far from being the law of progress, will always be in the direction of the *other* as *other*, even if the other is inferior : it will not be of necessity towards the more perfect.

But now observe : man is a material and not only a spiritual being, and according to the measure in which the life of the senses predominates in him over the life of the mind, the movement of humanity is subject to the conditions of matter : in this same measure the movement of humanity will be in the direction of the other as such, in the direction, that is, of the new, and not of the better. Look at them : they have only to possess a good to want something else ; truth wearies them : when by chance it is given them, they prefer to leave it to find novelty.

It is, then, the appetite of matter that lays hold of their heart, the taste of the dust of their origin that rises to their lips. Though the law of progress tends to dominate in history wherever the effort of the mind is able to succeed—especially in the order of knowledge and in the order of industrial technique—yet the law of human things is for the most part the law not of progress, but of alteration—the law of generation and corruption.

There is one human thing, it is true, that is an exception—the Church, which must grow and be made perfect to the fullness of the age of Christ, and which will know no decline. But that is precisely because it is not only human but divine, and it is animated by an omnipotent "form" which if it tolerates the imperfections of matter is never dominated by matter. In every other human society there follows decrepitude after growth, the alternation of lower forms and higher forms, the equilibrium of good and evil striking their balance in a variety of modes. But observe that the Church is not a foreign body isolated in the midst of humanity, but on the contrary the divinely formed organism into which the human race is called to enter that it may share in the Divine life. Hence arise singular complications which will be made clear only at the Last Judgement. In one measure, due to hidden and most mysterious solidarities between the Church and the world, the world, shaken in its very depths, will receive impulses coming from the law of growth which is proper to the Church and responds to the exigency of nature and of spirit; in another measure, it will be subject to the laws of ebb and flow, rise and fall, natural to human societies as such ; in still another, in so far as it seeks to separate itself from the Church and her influences, it will—like matter—know the law of disruption, the law of the old Adam. And all this will bear obvious fruit—to the eyes of the angels !—in history with its confused figures, its contradictions, the ambiguity of its unfolding.

Your error, most subtle Philonous, is an error that has reigned in metaphysics from the time of Descartes— the error of forgetting matter and the proper conditions of human nature. If man were a pure spirit and yet were evolving in time, his movement would be according to the dogma of necessary Progress. But man is but a rational animal and among the angels there is no evolution in time.[40]

The idea of necessary historic Progress is fundamentally as self-contradictory as the idea of a square circle. Historic Progress involves evolution in time, evolution in time involves matter : but matter involves a radical appetite for the new, an appetite not for the other as perfect, but for the other as other : hence the absence of necessary Progress or even of necessary tendency towards the more perfect. The myth of Progress is an excellent sample of the pseudo-idea, the idea which is at once " clear " for the imagination, and fundamentally absurd in itself.

THE MYTH OF
NECESSARY PROGRESS

THE MYTH OF NECESSARY PROGRESS

" In truth, I say, the omnibus is not only a vehicle on four wheels, it is the chariot of Progress, the symbol of peaceful association founded upon freedom."—EDMOND ABOUT.

" There will then come a moment upon this earth when the sun will shine upon none but free men who recognise no other master than their reason : when tyrants and slaves, priests and their stupid or hypocritical instruments, will exist no more save in history and on the stage."—CONDORCET.

" THE fundamental contradiction that you have brought to light, my dear Theonas, in the idea of the necessary Progress of humanity, surely bears with it a rabble of accessory contradictions, which make of this widely worshipped myth a tangle of absurdities ? " I said after a moment's silence, during which Philonous with a detached air watched the clouds drift by. " It seems odd, for example, that since it is founded almost solely upon Pascal's famous comparison of humanity with a growing man, those who hold it modestly abstain from remarking that in the individual man growth is followed by age and decay—and, thus modestly abstaining, they arrive at the conclusion that for humanity there is an endless progress in perfection."

THEONAS. What they do is simply to change their vocabulary when it comes to this point, and after all, since they are proceeding solely by way of analogy, nothing could be easier. They flit away from one kind of movement to another, abandon metaphors drawn from

117

the movement of growth to revel in those furnished by movement in space. Hence all the *stages* and *steps*, all the *ons* and *forwards*, all the *ascents*, *movements* and *élans* which contribute, if not to the enrichment, at any rate to the embellishment, of modern thought. Our friend Philonous must have in his repertoire many examples to illustrate my observation.

PHILONOUS. I would willingly quote you many if only you would show a little respect for what I hold in reverence.

> *Sur la terre, tantôt sable, tantôt savane,*
> *L'un à l'autre liés en longue caravane,*
> *Echangeant leur pensée en confuses rumeurs . . .*
> *Les esprits, voyageurs éternels, sont en marche.*
> *Ce saint voyage a nom Progrès.*

THEONAS. (Continuing the quotation.)

> *On avance toujours, on n'arrive jamais.*

PHILONOUS. So speaks the great poet of the age of democracy, whose profound genius as a thinker Charles Renouvier is almost the only man to have discovered. He says elsewhere,

> *Oh ! ce navire fait le voyage sacré !*
> *C'est l'ascension bleue à son premier degré . . .*
> *Il est le vaste élan du Progrès vers le ciel . . .*
> *Nef magique et suprême ! elle a, rien qu'en marchant,*
> *Changé le cri terrestre en pur et joyeux chant,*
> *Rajeuni les races flétries,*

Etabli l'ordre vrai, montré le chemin sûr,
Dieu juste ! et fait entrer dans l'homme tant d'azur
Qu'elle a supprimé les patries !

THEONAS. *Rien qu'en marchant* . . . simply by keeping moving . . . how very consoling.

PSEUDO-HYLAS. I remember a worthy Russian Social Democrat whom I knew in the long ago ; nourished upon a decoction of Spencer and Marx sugared with Pierre Lavroff, he used to evoke, his eyes swimming in ecstasy, the man driving from stage to stage, his hand on the wheel of the motor-car of history, in virtue of an inevitable evolutionary process, to the achievement of his destiny . . .

But notice in the characteristic example of the verses quoted by our friend, how the *idea-feeling* works. A man reading the verses receives absolutely nothing in the intellect ; yet a vague flood of generous emotions pours in to stir his heart and set his bosom heaving : and he asks himself how could anything not be true which so sets his better self a-quiver ? This is what we mean when we speak of judging according to the appetite of the subject instead of judging according to the object. And this sort of voluntary self-deception explains a very large part of the success in the modern world, especially among women, of the " consoling " philosophies of sentiment or intuition—observe for example the seductive fascination exercised over weak minds by that ethical idealism at bargain prices in which spiritualism and theosophy wrap their unhealthy rubbish.

THEONAS. Notice also the service rendered to the muse

of Progress Without End, by movement in space. If Victor Hugo had borrowed his images from the movement of accretion, it would have been difficult to exalt us by the picture of a microbe for example, turning into a mammal and swelling till it reached the sky. The movement in space on the other hand, by the very fact that it affects the subject only extrinsically, lends itself most admirably to being prolonged indefinitely.

And at this point there comes to light a fresh contradiction in the myth of Progress. Progress, as it is conceived by its worshippers, is essentially progress to *infinity*, without end, and this because if we place ourselves in imagination at any point in the future, no matter how distant, the law of necessary Progress, dominating history with metaphysical necessity, must continue to be in action and to demand in consequence new degrees of perfection. Yet on the other hand it is so impossible for desire to reach out to anything save towards a good or an end, that this same Progress must necessarily suppose tendency *towards an end*—otherwise it would fall into the gulf of non-existence from the complete cessation of human effort. That is why, after having most definitely stated that one always advances but never arrives—that is that the voyage has no end—our poet immediately adds that his troop goes on without for one single instant losing sight of

Le terme du voyage et l'asile où l'on tend,

to wit, " holy liberty " and " the universal Hymen." Is not that so ?

PHILONOUS. Quite true. And I am pleased to observe

that you study our authors. But the contradiction which you think you have discovered, straightens out very easily. The great minds, the bearers of civilisation, the philosophers, know that Progress is indefinite because there is no term and no goal of any sort for anything—that *Becoming* alone is self-sufficient. But the people they are trying to teach do not know it : these die joyfully for Progress, because they firmly believe, each time that the Past falls away from them, that they are about to attain the goal of their desires, to grasp with their hands the happiness that we promise them. For we do promise it, with a loving, almost a priestly, heart, certain that thereby we are co-operating with the divine powers and accelerating the onward movement of the universe. Oh hallowed illusion of the simple, hidden spring of the world and of the world's Progress, how can we refuse to lap you round with our enlightened care !

THEONAS. Please do not try to play Dr. Faustus : the *rôle* does not suit your innocent heart.

PHILONOUS. You don't know how great is the soul capacity of an idealist philosopher.

THEONAS. Oh I do, I do ! At least in part.

PHILONOUS My old friend Père Malebranche who was somewhat excitable and with whom I had several acrimonious discussions—he was a mighty defender of reason !—anyhow on one occasion he very nearly quarrelled with me because I forgot myself and wrote poetry :

it was in mockery of my lyrical effort that he composed his famous distich :

> *Il fait en ce beau jour le plus beau temps du monde*
> *Pour aller à cheval sur la terre et sur l'onde.* . . .

THEONAS. To his way of thinking, poetry was so much nonsense, prose alone was rational : yet for all that, the Abbé Faydit wrote of him : " He sees all things in God, yet does not see that he is a fool," and Bossuet came down upon him heavily for all the nonsense he wrote in theology. . . .

PHILONOUS. I remember that Père Malebranche used to thrash his dog as hard as he could in honour of Descartes' theory that animals are only machines. " Notice," he would say, " the dog cries but does not feel." Personally, in my moments of pessimism I should like to flog the whole human race when I see the senseless obstacles that it puts in the way of the law of Progress, which yet *must* take place. I understand in those moments how the great artificers of Progress, the great benefactors of humanity, had recourse to fire and steel and every form of violence.

THEONAS. My dear fellow, you positively alarm me.

PHILONOUS. I alarm myself. At such moments it seems to me that I differ from Lenin—another great lover of men, as Maxim Gorki has so touchingly told us—only by a certain lack of military spirit : I would almost say, in fact I *would* say, by a certain timidity in carrying out what I feel : for really I *feel* the same, sometimes. Fortunately the trusty principles of my unswerving liberalism have me in their care, and I recover quickly.

THEONAS. Very well, recover now ! and let us proceed together to strip the bark from the idea of necessary Progress. I *think* that I see a curious contradiction in this idea. Do you mind helping me to track it down ?

PHILONOUS. If you like ; but I don't think you will convince me.

THEONAS. Well, you agree that the repairing of a house presupposes that the foundations already laid are not changed and that new materials are added to the old without destroying the old ? And that likewise the growth of an organism presupposes that the plan of construction, directing the development from the earliest stages of the embryo, does not change—that growth demands the incorporation, as it were, of new matter with the old ?

PHILONOUS. Granted.

THEONAS. And will you agree that knowledge grows in a mind—whether by extension to fresh objects and further conclusions, or by a strengthening and intensification of what it already knows about a particular object—only if the principles of that knowledge remain firm in the mind and the new stages acquired *remain* acquired ?

PHILONOUS. Obviously.

123

THEONAS. Therefore we must say that every change which perfects the subject, all progress in fact, demands that the future should conserve, in one way or another, the gains acquired by the past.

PHILONOUS. I have never thought otherwise ; and I like to find the true motto of Progress in the maxim : *vetera novis augere.*

THEONAS. Very well then ; if the law of Progress is, as you think, a metaphysically necessary law of human history—if not actually of the whole of nature and the essence of things—then its domain must be universal and nothing, absolutely nothing, can escape it.

PHILONOUS. It would seem that that must be so, oh wise Theonas !

THEONAS. Therefore there is absolutely nothing of the past which is not less good than the present, and this, in its turn, is less good than the future ?

PHILONOUS. That is the logical conclusion.

THEONAS. From which it follows that if anything of the past subsists in the present and claims to subsist in the future, it is an evil, a thing intolerable ?

PHILONOUS. Good. I am a worshipper of *becoming*.

THEONAS. The law of Progress then, demands for its full realisation the destruction of all that comes from the past ? . . . Answer, my dear Sir ; do not be afraid. After all, your poet has already set a courageous example. See with how sure a sense of the benefits of destruction he choses a guide who " at each stage " takes the head of his caravan :

> *Quand Jean Huss disparaît, Luther pensif se montre,*
> *Luther s'en va, Voltaire alors prend le flambeau,*
> *Quand Voltaire s'arrête, arrive Mirabeau.*

Remember in particular the beautiful honesty with which he affirms, as a truth immediately evident, the identity of Evil and the Past, an identity so complete that in one place he rolls these two synonyms into one, as the single subject of an eloquent outburst :

> *C'est l'instant ou le* Mal, *prenant toutes les formes* . . .
> *C'est l'heure ou le* Passé, *qu'ils laissent derrière eux,*
> *Voyant dans chacun d'eux une proie échappée,*
> *Surprend la caravane assoupie et campée.* . . .

By a logical and inevitable process the myth of necessary Progress thus leads to a sort of grotesque Manicheeism— a chronological Manicheeism, if I dare coin such a phrase —in which the fleeting line of the present, the *nunc fluens*, separates the luminous realm of the Good—that is the Future—from the dark domain of Evil—that is the Past : and the Past, alas, eternally gnaws into the Good and as it were swallows its first beginnings at every round of the sun-dial—since by a deplorable fate, a little of the Future becomes at every moment the Present, and then the Past.

PHILONOUS. It is all very well for you to father your barbarous mythology on other people : I absolutely refuse to recognise in it the ideas I love.

THEONAS. Examine your conscience, gaze deeply into your hidden tendencies, soon you will discern the moving shadow of this mythology deep in the background of all your modern prejudices. Alas, it is almost impossible to conceive the mighty place, the utterly monstrous place, that it holds in our subconscious these two centuries past. It is to that that a powerful mind like Auguste Comte owes most of his weaknesses. He never shook himself free of it though he did very clearly discern certain characteristics of real progress : in particular he recognised that no real progress can be indefinite, and that all real progress presupposes the conservation of what is good in the past. It was the myth of necessary Progress that underlay his law of the Three States ; it was under its influence that Comte, like Saint-Simon, regarded the French Revolution as the irreversible coming to realisation of a New Jerusalem, whose religion it was reserved to him to found. Above all it is this—this idea that the future must always as such be better than the past—this and perhaps only this, that has always prevented those who hold it from envisaging the bare possibility of minds returning to the Catholic religion. " To re-establish the Catholic order," he wrote one day with bewildering *naïveté*, " it would be necessary to suppress the philosophy of the eighteenth century, and as this philosophy proceeds from the Reformation, and Luther's Reformation in its turn was but the result of the experimental sciences introduced into Europe by the Arabs, it would be necessary to suppress the sciences ! " That surely is a perfect text, I know it by heart : and it illustrates—as clearly as the historico-economic syntheses of Karl Marx—what havoc the myth of Progress can work in the mind of an intelligent man. And what of Marx? What of Marx's master, Hegel?

But let us come back to our discussion, and to the self-destructive implications of the myth of Progress. Another line of thought will perhaps bring us to the same conclusions that you hesitated to admit a moment ago. Progress means change. As Progress is absolutely necessary and the law of Progress has, as we have seen, an absolutely universal domain, the things that we call foundations and principles—whether in the order of knowledge or in the order of the moral life—must absolutely change like everything else.

PHILONOUS. Certainly.

THEONAS. But the foundations being changed, all that rested on them must break down?

PHILONOUS. It would seem so.

THEONAS. But then it follows that since the law of Progress demands the ceaseless changing of the foundations and principles admitted in the past, it also demands that the movement of humanity towards the Better must take place by means of a process of breaking down and radical destruction, everlastingly repeated.

PHILONOUS. Well, yes : if you like, I grant that.

THEONAS. We shall then have to say that progress, as progress, demands some kind of conservation of the gains acquired by the past ; but we shall also have to say that

Necessary Progress, in as much as it expresses a law which you claim to be metaphysically necessary and universal in its operation, demands the regular destruction and disappearance of these same gains. Thus real progress is devoured by Progress, the idea-myth.

PHILONOUS. I admit that I can find no flaw in the links of your argument. But that does not affect my conviction that you are wrong.

THEONAS. Here we are at the Heritage again. Shall we go in? We can continue the conversation when you have rested a little.

THE PHILOSOPHY OF REVOLUTION

THE PHILOSOPHY OF REVOLUTION

" A little while, a reflection : . . . and an immense movement will be born, a new era will open : an era of amaze for the crowd, of surprise and terror for tyrants, of liberation for a great people and hope for the earth."—
VOLNEY.

" HERE is bread, milk, honey from my hives," said Theonas when we had entered, " restore your strength and let us thank God for the good things that He offers us as remedy for the weakness of our nature. When St. Paul the Hermit, at the age of 113, received a visit from the nonagenarian St. Anthony, the two solitaries ate with much giving of thanks the whole loaf brought that day by the faithful crow which for sixty years had brought St. Paul every day the half of a loaf. We read likewise in Cassian's second Conference with the Abbot Moses, that to do honour to his guests Moses shared with them at the hour of Vespers one of the two little loaves which were the food of his day. But we must conform our frugality to the demands of a climate less easy than that of the desert of Scete."

" Oh ! " replied Philonous, " three and a half grams of bread are enough for me. Chewing them for half an hour—according to Fletcher's method of three thousand mastications per mouthful—I shall be quite satisfied. You know, of course, that Fletcherism, which has found its natural allies among the Adventists and is now incorporated in their religion, stands at the present moment as one of the great scientific movements by means of which America has undertaken to bring about the regeneration of the human species. Horace Fletcher, propagator and apostle of integral mastication, and author of *The New Glutton or Epicure*, reduced his daily ration to thirty mouthfuls of food. After a few years of this *régime* he was able, we are told, ' to cycle a hundred miles a day, to go through the movement of bending and stretching—before witnesses—up to five thousand times a day, though this movement for most people is fatiguing after a dozen repetitions. . . .' "

THEONAS. Where do you read these edifying details ?

PHILONOUS. In a book written by M. Wincenty Lutoslawski of the University of Geneva. Ah ! my friends, to what a sovereign height will not science elevate man in that day when it comes into plenary possession of the hallowed laws of Hygiene, so that all our functions of assimilation, growth and reproduction shall be regulated by those laws ! It maddens me that I was not born two hundred years later. But, even as it is, all our ancestors seem to me like so many anthropoids of a rudimentary and unclean animalism. Your solitaries of Middle Egypt, totally ignorant of eugenic hygiene and ordering their sobriety to some vague spiritual ends, were but pallid precursors, shadowy paleo-fletcherites. I am pretty sure that their mastication was very imperfect. Even the great Descartes, when he expected from science the attainment " of the highest degree of perfection of which our nature is capable," and the indefinite prolongation of human life, yet did not have the remotest suspicion of the way in which this idea would germinate in America, or of the free and joyous simplification that the notion of science was to undergo—still less of the cures of Mrs. Eddy and the five thousand bendings and stretchings of Horace Fletcher.

THEONAS. It looks to me as though we had got back again to our original subject, the adorable idea of Progress.

PHILONOUS. Your philosophy can say what it likes : never will the instinct of progress quit the heart of man.

THEONAS. I agree. It is the instinct of the mind itself in its conflict with matter. But we claim that the so-called law of necessary Progress, otherwise called the Dogma of Progress, works precisely—and almost laughably—towards the frustration of that instinct. For real progress is essentially conservative of the gains made by it, essentially positive : while Progress according to the dogma is essentially destructive or negative.

PHILONOUS. Your arguments are fallacies, and I can prove it by an unanswerable objection.

THEONAS. Let us hear it.

PHILONOUS. It pleases you, apparently, to contrast Progress and revolution, and you have put me in a certain difficulty by tricking me into agreeing that the contrast is legitimate. But I now see that that is the very thing I should have denied ! I now declare that revolution as such is a good thing, fertile of good. When the chicken breaks the shell of his egg, he makes a revolution. Every new form and every new school of art is revolutionary in relation to that which has gone before it : we were reminded recently that Malherbe one day showed Philippe Desportes a copy of the works of Ronsard from which he had himself scratched out every line. Those Middle Ages which you admire so enthusiastically made no bones about throwing over roman for gothic and the old style for the *dolce stil nuovo :* was not St. Thomas Aquinas praised by his biographer Guglielmo de Tocco for the novelty of his teaching and very definitely not praised by the adherents of the older scholasticism, who held him to be a revolutionary ? Why, wasn't it St. Paul who said that when one becomes a man, one puts away the things of a child ? And that is a revolution. Thus there is no Progress save by way of revolution.

THEONAS. Your examples are very good, but you are constructing a syllogism in four terms : for the word revolution has two different meanings. Sometimes it means a radical change, primarily destructive and due to a victory of matter—as in the " eruptions " and " earthquakes " so popular in revolutionary literature : *La raison tonne en son cratère. . . .*

PHILONOUS (*sings*). *C'est l'éruption de la fin.*

THEONAS. Sometimes it means a radical change, but primarily constructive and due to a victory of spirit, as in the examples you have just urged against me. From the mere fact that changes of the first sort are more external and visible, it follows that the popular sense of the word " revolution " would tend to be confined to them : further, from these same changes, the myth of Necessary Progress borrowed the substance of its fellow-myth of Revolution Personified. Whereas the revolutions you speak of are profound changes, certainly, but by way of positive development or perfecting.

They do not destroy what the past has gained, rather they confirm it, and preserve it. For to the eye that can see beneath appearances, the very substance of the past—brought to greater perfection—is found in such cases in a new state or a new form. All the sap of the tradition of St. Augustine is in St. Thomas ; all the human values of the child are in the adult—who puts away only what is peculiar to the state of childhood as such ; all that faith believes will be seen in glory. And it is the same—at least in essence and in principle, if not in the totality of the good things of the past—for scientific and artistic revolutions when these really do mark progress. What was true in the Ptolemaic astronomy survived in the Copernican revolution ; and though in my eyes the old Satyr of the Vendôme who

destourna d'Hélicon les Muses en la France

deserved better of poetry than the wise Norman

qui réduisit la Muse aux règles du devoir

yet it is true to say—as was said in reply to M. de La Tailhède by a journalist whose name I have forgotten—that the art of Malherbe and his school did very notably absorb and assimilate much of the essential spirit of Ronsard.

PHILONOUS. Degas said of a famous painter at the time of his election to the Académie des Beaux-Arts : " He is a hermit who knows the times of the trains." I see in you, my dear Theonas, a hermit who reads the newspapers and the reviews. You are more modern than you look.

THEONAS. Hermits, you must know, have always been, of all men, the best informed upon the things of the world. As they have their heart in eternity, and eternity is in contact with the whole course of time at every point, it follows that they must also be of the present day. But we may now draw to light another characteristic of the fecund revolutions of which you have given examples. They are the term of a longer or shorter movement of progression, and thus—despite secondary conflicts—they presuppose as the very condition of their being an underlying continuity of life and activity.

PHILONOUS. Yet they do not take place, ordinarily, without loss and damage.

THEONAS. But the damage is accidental, a point which must never be forgotten.

To understand the matter more profoundly and more philosophically, notice this : that as the word " progress " evokes the image of continuous movement, so the word " revolution " evokes—more or less remotely, with the deficiencies common to metaphorical analogies—the image of the movement of generation and corruption, in which one form—using the word as it is used in metaphysics—gives place to another, and which does in fact constitute the term of a continuous movement.

Now you know what Aristotle says : *generatio unius*

corruptio alterius. The production of the plant is bound up with the corruption of the seed, the destruction of a man is bound up with the production of cadaveric fermentations and their chemical residues. There is no destruction that does not produce something, no production that does not destroy some existent thing. The whole question is to know whether it is the production or the destruction that is the principal event : that is to say, whether one passes from a lower form to a higher, or inversely—whether we are in the presence of the change that makes a living body or of the change that makes a heap of corruption.

Consider for a moment the Russian revolution. It is right to denounce the immense destructions wrought by it : yet the friends of Bolshevism would not be wrong in declaring the argument inadequate and in heroically accepting blood and ruins, if all these disasters opened the way, as they imagine, to a better world : the death of God upon Calvary was a more frightful tragedy. Their error is that they do not see the infra-human and anti-human baseness of the forms generated by these immense destructions.

It is puerile to imagine that in material nature some evil is not bound up with good accidentally, and that among men any splendid thing can arise without some defect. But it is absurd to think—and this is the sin of revolutionary romanticism—that a radical upheaval and destruction are the condition of *all* Progress, that cataclysm of itself produces a better state.

PHILONOUS. All this requires many distinctions and piercing discernment.

THEONAS. It requires that those who judge of human things should use their intelligence. The trouble is that they rarely do. The merely conservative ones take all newness for a newness of corruption—thus, to choose an example in the intellectual order, Etienne Tempier, Bishop of Paris, condemned with all due magnificence, in the name of tradition, certain theses of Thomas Aquinas exactly three years after his death, the 7th of March, 1277, never suspecting that by a most piquant stroke of divine irony that same day, the 7th of March, would remain consecrated to the Doctor for the celebration of his sanctity. On the other hand, the mystics of Revolution take all newness for a newness of achievement or perfection, and condemn the whole of the past in the name of Necessary Progress, not seeing that they are thus destroying all possibility of real progress and fruitful revolution, together with all means of profiting by what is solid in the new things acquired in the past.

Truly it is not the professed revolutionaries that make the most profound revolutions.

God, says Dionysius the Areopagite, is called a Zealot because of His great love for all that is. Those who work with God have, like Him, a passion for what is, for being. They attach themselves passionately to all the lineaments of being, to all that bears trace and hope of life. If, after that, a world grown cheap like the modern world, ends up by breaking down in ruin, it is of small importance to them : they only want to save what subsists in it of human and divine value : and that, in truth, will be saved.

We are not afraid of revolution, my dear Philonous. It is we, at the end of all things, who will bring it to pass.

For we realise that the world as it is is condemned, and that the temporal salvation of humanity depends upon a revolution far more radical than any envisaged by dialectical materialism : for it must begin in the heart, and it must change the very principles of our civilisation.

PHILONOUS. You are frightfully arrogant. You forget that you yourselves made those very revolutions which you attack as destructive—I mean that they derive, indirectly I grant, from that Christianity which you profess to serve. All revolutionary ideas are, in their origin, Christian ideas : there is no more revolutionary idea than to propose to men as their first law that they must love one another.

THEONAS. Pardon me, but it is not the first law, it is the second. The first commandment is to love God above all things : to love God and therefore to love the order willed by God in the world of nature as in the world of grace—I am not forgetting that order is realised in human societies in different and changing modes. Yet you are right in one sense. The so-called revolutionary ideas are not Christian ideas, but they are corruptions of Christian ideas. From this point of view, it is true to say that the religion of Revolution can invent nothing and has had to borrow everything from its old enemy Christianity. Its myths of *Humanity* and of the *City of the Future*, are simply the ideas of the Church and of the heavenly Jerusalem, fallen from the divine plane to the earthly ; *Revolution* itself is conceived as a sort of Last Judgement ; the *Regeneration* of the human species set as the goal of our hopes is a poor shadow of baptismal regeneration. And as for *Necessary Progress*, it is simply an unhappy substitute for Providence. The general process of scaling down and degradation to which Christian ideas have been subjected in modern times. . . .

PHILONOUS. I do not quite see why.

THEONAS. The reason is quite clear. Christianity preserves its essence and its life only in the Church. The divorce of Christianity from the Church, which began with the Reformation, had, as direct consequence, a beginning of corruption for Christianity.

PHILONOUS. In what does this corruption consist, according to you ?

THEONAS. Just imagine what Christian values can become when men cease to believe in the supernatural order, in the supernaturalness of grace, which is the soul of Christianity ! What you had first was a *naturalising* corruption, a reduction of the Gospel to the plane of nature. One can see what must have been the immediate effects of this from the point of view of our present discussion.

The order of grace is *other* than that of nature, but being *supernatural* it perfects it and does not destroy it. But if you regard what is of grace as natural—and at the same time try to preserve the shadow of it thus left, and impose it upon things—then what you are really doing is trying violently to *substitute* another order for the order of nature : and so you destroy the natural order in the name of a divine principle and a divine virtue : there you have the whole mystical basis of Revolution. The passion for Justice and for Mercy, the consciousness that all our human hierarchies are nothing in face of God, the feeling that we are made for a divine destiny, the immense reversal of values taught by the Gospel—the exaltation of the humble and the mighty made low : all this finds a marvellously harmonious realisation in the supernatural order of grace—and at the same time radiates through the whole order of human things, to elevate it and bring it peace, to vivify and not to destroy it ; but fallen to the plane of the dreams and demands of pure nature, it becomes only a zeal for revolutionary Messianism.[41] That is why Jean-Jacques Rousseau, who completed what Luther had begun—the divorce of Christianity from the Church *and* from its necessary connection with the supernatural—is truly the Father of the modern world, in so far as it is a world of humanism centred upon man.

PHILONOUS. Yet he did not believe in progress.

THEONAS. It is true that the dogma of Progress has other origins ; even if we do not trace it right back to Descartes, we can see it arising in thinkers as profound as Volney, Condorcet, Turgot . . . but in actual fact Rousseau's polemic against the philosophers was of no effect with regard to this dogma. On the contrary, Rousseauism entered perfectly into harmony with it and was a most powerful aid to its successful sweep.

PHILONOUS. How ?

THEONAS. The really important point in Rousseau's principle of natural goodness—which is only a translation into natural terms of the Christian dogma of Original Innocence—is not that he placed his philosophic paradise at the beginning of human history, but that he regarded the perfections of that paradise—its leisure, innocence, perfect liberty, earthly beatitude—as conditions of a state *due* to human nature and demanded by it. It followed that since this state did not actually exist in the present and yet *should* by right of nature exist, it must of necessity be an affair of the future to bring us to possess it. *Emile* and the *Contrat social*, whatever Rousseau may have thought himself, are the breviary of the education and the society of the future. By a fatal displacement, the state of natural goodness is set at the term of human history, as its necessary result : so that our very essence constrains us to appeal without ceasing—with the impatience of the prophets longing for the Messiah—from the present to the future. Thus the whole force of Rousseau's fallacy came in the end as a most potent aid to the dogma of Progress.

For us Christians, on the other hand, the state of original perfection was not due to human nature : it was a gratuitous privilege ; our nature as such has a right to the earth and its labours—an earth less dark and labours less hard if nature had not been wounded—it has no right to paradise.

PHILONOUS. Then we must say that all is for the best in the best of all possible worlds, and that society in its present state is the best that can be hoped for here below ! So long as order reigns, all is well !

THEONAS. So cruel and so bitter do we find the world

of fallen humanity that for our consolation *nothing* will suffice save the certain expectation of the resurrection of the dead. As to order—if it were good as such, then any order would do—there is order among the demons : in truth, a despotic order that violates the eternal laws is a disorder crying to heaven for vengeance. And as to modern society, the accusations we can bring against it are immeasurably stronger than yours, for we know that it wrongs not only man but God.

Yet human nature is what it is : we are a species naturally wretched—since evil comes to us more often than good. Therefore we must recognise not only the degrees, the inequalities, the limitations of every sort that the order of nature and justice demand : we must also recognise that abuses and defects beyond number, sins of malice and more sins of stupidity—a certain dose of injustice, in a word—will always be mixed in with the things of man. We must not make Rousseau's mistake of rejecting the conditions essential to life and human society because of the injustice which is found joined with them by accident.

PHILONOUS. You Catholics are easily resigned to injustice.

THEONAS. Human cowardice is great, my friend, among Catholics as among other men—greater even among Catholics when they are slack, as so many are in our day. After all, you would not say what you have just said if you were better informed upon the life of the Church and its doctrine. *Societas conservari non potest sine justitia*, is, for the Church, axiomatic. "Woe to him,"

143

cries St. Catherine of Sienna, "who does not see that the great conserving force is holy justice." "He who is not corrected or does not correct is like a limb that begins to decay. . . ." It is because of its injustice, its very gross injustice, that the world of classic humanism has become the decomposing thing in the midst of which we are trying to advance. Christians, my dear Philonous, hate injustice precisely in the measure in which they love God. And, as I have already suggested, we hate it more deeply than the humanitarians because we know that it has supernatural repercussions. *They* claim to strive against it as though it was their mission to govern the universe and to make absolute justice reign therein ; and seeking justice outside the ways that God has set, they do not augment justice. But we, we strive against it, each within the limits of the power apportioned to us, like subordinates who carry out the parts of a plan of which it is not for them to judge, of which they do not know the totality. And more than that—we know that the first injustice to be repressed is our own, for we have been told to seek first the kingdom of God which is within ; and when we have truly laboured, still in the evening we have our sacrifice, our suffering to offer in reparation. Whenever we have neglected this strife, we have been sternly punished.

PHILONOUS. We must believe, then, that these instances of neglect have been fairly frequent in the course of history ?

THEONAS. True. And I wonder if the immense development of the religion of revolution and the false zeal for justice do not correspond with great exactitude to our own fallings away from true justice. We do not think enough of the terrible march of the justice of God through human history. There are certain effects of justice demanded by the deepest laws of the equilibrium of Being, which one would say that God will have at all costs : if He does not find saints who procure these effects in mercy, He charges men in revolt to procure them in ruins. . . . Likewise among those who hate us— if in the obscurity of their heart it is not that they hate us, but that they truly love justice—there are some who are nearer to us than they think, or than we think.

" Well put," said Philonous, turning to me. " But I see quite well that it would be waste of time to put before Theonas the object of my visit, the idea of a Union of Hermits of which I was speaking to you as we came along. I am afraid there is nothing to be done with hermits."

THE PROGRESS OF THE SPIRIT

THE PROGRESS OF THE SPIRIT

" The belief in Progress is a doctrine of the slothful. . . . True civiliza-
tion is not a matter of gas or steam or table turning. It consists in the
lessening of the effects of original sin."—BAUDELAIRE.

" It is to industry that we shall one day owe that we are all enlightened
and all honest. It will make men without prejudices and without vices
as it has created bulls without horns : the miracle would not be greater."—
EDMOND ABOUT.

THEONAS. Night is falling, my dear friends, and we
must soon bring our discussion to a close. I should like
to return to the subject with which we began. I see a
whole series of closely linked conclusions to be drawn
from the principles which seem to us to dominate the
question of Progress, and I should like to draw them out
for you.

We said that everything in this matter arises from the
fact that man is essentially composite, and that in this
strange union of a spiritual " form " and a material
principle of sheer mutability, the natural tendency of
the spirit towards that which is more perfect conflicts
inevitably with the natural appetite of matter for whatever
is new, for the other as other : so that the idea of Necessary
Progress makes no sense, since the law of *progress*—that is
change for the better—and the law of *mere change* are
everywhere intertwined in us. Understand me aright.
I do not deny that men are capable of progress or even
that they are made for progress : but I say that it is
absurd to think that progress is to be achieved *necessarily*,
in virtue of some divine spring or of a metaphysical law

of human history. It is absurd precisely because man is a perfectible being—and hence, being perfectible, necessarily corruptible also. His specific difference—that in him which constitutes him a species different from others —is involved in this. Between mere sense intuition and the pure intellection proper to the angels, lies the mind of the *animal that reasons*—by nature bound down to logical movement as his body is submitted to movements ruled by the laws of matter : and thus, as he can and should be perfect, he can also deteriorate : a fact clamourously obvious to common-sense, yet simply not grasped by the devotees of Progress.

Nowhere does this condition of the human creature appear more strongly marked than in the moral life of the individual. Nowhere does one more clearly see that progress is not *necessary*—that is to say that it does not take place *necessarily*. And nowhere does one see more clearly that progress is a necessity for us, in this sense that we are obliged to make endless progress if we are not to fall. For every activity, if it tends less towards perfection than the virtue from which it emanates, will tend to diminish this virtue.

There is no rest for us : so far the " mobilism " of the Bergsonians is right. Held in the strong grasp of sovereign Mercy, the biting whip of Time scourges us without ceasing. " Go, child of God, go." What her voices said to Joan of Arc, each moment says to the soul. The *castle* of St. Teresa is a castle of wind and of flame. Doubtless the saints remain most tranquil in their images. But if we would picture to ourselves the soul of the saints, we should have to imagine a sort of great hurricane—yet a hurricane obedient to, and governed in its movement by, the wings of the eagle of the Spirit, a hurricane whirling upwards unceasingly to God. That is the only progress that can compensate for the trouble of living. *Ascensiones in corde disposuit.*

PHILONOUS. My dear fellow, in our busy modern world we cannot spare the time to think of that sort of progress. Can you see us planted in the street, our eyes raised to heaven like the apostles after the Ascension ? " *Quid statis adspicientes in cœlum ?* " A friendly policeman, an earthly sort of angel, would say, " Come along now, move on." I know that Max Jacob claims, in his *Défense de Tartufe*, to have had heavenly apparitions at the cinema. But I should be disposed to regard that as, on the whole, an extraordinary way. No, what we are interested in is not vertical movement, the progress of the soul upwards towards some heavenly object, but horizontal movement, the progress of humanity here below towards the perfection of its natural activity. Tell us something about that.

THEONAS. I was just about to do so. Must we not say that where the effort of the spirit is least hampered by matter and finds its own success most easily, there also— and only—will the law of progress tend to dominate ? All we have to do now is to let this principle develop its consequences.

If it is a question of minor victories over inert matter, we are easily more cunning than matter : also in the order of material making, progress will be the rule—not only progress but indefinite progress, at least within the limits of one continuous period—for after the great breaches of historical continuity everything, or practically everything, has had to begin again : think of the lost arts of the Hittites or the ancient Egyptians.

It is from this field of material making that popular imagination borrows its notion of progress : and principally it sees it as something like the increasing rapidity of means of transport—for here also is verified the definition of progress proposed by those learned men who call it " economy of energy." [42] Progress of this order has held the stage for roughly a century with a shower of marvels, and the fascination exercised by it has certainly served more than anything else to create the prestige that the dogma of Progress has among men. It would be waste of time to remind you that of itself it contributes nothing either to the moral perfection of men nor even to their earthly happiness—since concupiscence is limitless and human needs grow faster than the means of satisfying them. What is more important, this purely material progress—good of course in its own order, but definitely of a low order—puts civilisation in presence of a measureless peril since it throws human life off its axis and sets ever more powerful means to the service of a creature feeble and perverse. If it definitively took the preponderance and the directing rôle, it would mean for the West decadence beyond remedy.

PHILONOUS. At any rate, one thing remains—the progress you speak of leads to a general diminution of suffering.

THEONAS. You mean the Great War ?

PHILONOUS. You are now arguing from an accident. The war was a catastrophe. . . .

THEONAS. Quite true : yet it had its causes, and its most immediate causes were linked very definitely with that mindless predominance of material activity.

PHILONOUS. Leave that aside. You will not deny the relief brought to human suffering by the great medical discoveries ? Antisepsis, Anæsthesis, Serotherapy, Physiotherapy, Opotherapy. . . . Prophylaxis and scientific disinfection, as we were reminded by M. Léon Lafitte in an article in the *Mercure de France*, have reduced enormously the ravages of typhoid fever, eruptive fevers, diphtheria, puerperal fever, and have practically banished cholera, the plague, yellow fever, typhus.

THEONAS. They have not done much against Spanish 'flu. In proportion as we triumph over the evils which now afflict us, new evils arise.

PHILONOUS. Yes, but the evils overcome are none the less overcome !

THEONAS. I quite agree : and what I have said in no way reflects on the merit and the genius of those who have shown us how to overcome them. But it is possible that their discoveries—and in general the relief of pain and the greater ease in ordinary life which science has brought us—do no more than make up for the increase of sufferings in another order for which our civilisation is responsible —with the net result that the average suffering of humanity remains pretty well the same at all times.

The truth is that we are not here to avoid suffering, but rather to put it to good use.

153

PHILONOUS. Spoken like a virtuous hermit. But please resume the thread of those deductions which you were proposing to set before us.

THEONAS. I was saying that in the field of mere making, of production, industry and the practical sciences, progress must be the rule. In the field of the moral life, however, there is no unvarying progress for humanity, but endless vicissitudes : because matter—our own animated matter—is hard to control.

Doubtless civilisation—*de jure* at least—has primarily a moral end, since it is ordered to the *totum bene vivere* of the human being, and a right moral life is the essential thing in this *bene vivere*. Therefore, in the developing of all our activities, civilisation tends—provided the development is normal—to bring us back to our Principle, and this according to the great thought of the older philosophers, is the very definition of true progress. But in fact there is such a falling-short that it is not difficult to understand the reactionary furies of a Rousseau or a Tolstoy—inapt, both of them, to distinguish the essential from the accidental, particularly when the accidental is very voluminous. A result of this falling-short is that the moral advantages of civilisation—save where a superhuman leaven leavens the whole lump—seem to profit only a small number. Finally—and especially—it is certain that the great flowerings of civilisation, with their miracles of human productivity, are not the general law, but only high points of achievement, fortunate certainly, but difficult and exceptional : and their decadence and corruption are worse than barbarism. No, Necessary Progress is not to be looked for there.

PHILONOUS. And the advent of Christianity ? Are you going to deny that there, at any rate, was an immense moral progress ?

THEONAS. Christianity is a divine fact, and gratuitous : it is not a *natural* progress of humanity. When the theorizers of Progress—from the priest-philosophers of the eighteenth century down to Herder—use it as an example, they are playing an unworthy trick upon their public.

Besides, if Christianity, by the slow diffusion of its influence amongst the mass of men, has, in fact, brought about general improvements of profound importance— such as the abolition of slavery—and has everywhere brought about a new scale of values : and if, till the end of the world, it must of necessity powerfully transfigure the world : yet the true and proper field of activity of its virtues is *not* the general mass of men but primarily and principally the Mystical Body of Christ. There, and only there, do we find a glorious unbroken progress manifesting the power of the spirit ; there, and only there, does humanity—in the measure in which it lives the life of the Church—rise above itself. Doubtless, in the historical development of the Church, the ages closer to the Beginning, closer to the Passion and to Pentecost received the more sublime out-pouring—the epistles of St. Paul, for example, are more divine than the *Summa Theologica.* Yet only at the end will the Body in its completeness have its perfect differentiation and the totality of its number : and it must grow till then. But there is the other side of the picture : humanity continues to be directed in its movement towards a divine goal unknown to itself ; yet if it breaks with the life of the Church it makes its own wounds worse than if Christ had not come. *Si non venissem, et locutus fuissem eis, peccatum non haberent.* Never forget that the same light that lightens some blinds others. Thus what is of the world descends, while what is of the spirit rises—a truth that you may compare with M. Bergson's *élan créateur* energising amidst the downward movement of matter.

So much for the field of human *action*, or morality, which has its source principally in the will.

PHILONOUS. Good : now tell us of that which constitutes the more special field of the intellect.

THEONAS. In the fine arts, which are the most purely intellectual fruits of the *operative* intelligence, it is not progress that reigns, but change—I mean a certain law of renewal and innovation. Why ? Because the artist's special task is to incarnate beauty in a determinate piece of matter, and because matter is immeasurably poverty-stricken by comparison with beauty : so that every form of art, however noble it be, is destined ultimately to wear out and yield place to another. I know that on the side of technique art involves a certain progress, just in so far as technique supposes tradition, teaching, human collaboration, across the ages. But as the progressive establishment of traditions of technique demands only the simplest conditions of intellectual and social life these traditions may very well be quite adequately constituted in the very earliest ages of civilisations ; and therefore, the passage of time may in this order bring changes, but not necessarily progress—nay, it may even bring regress as, for example, happened to us at the end of the eighteenth century, with its totally retrograde abandonment of those same traditions.

And there is this further point : if technique—and with it all that mass of secondary matter of which art has need—demands that the artist should have a master and take his place in a tradition, yet art itself, most formally *as* art, in the conception of its product as creation, belongs to the *via inventionis*—in other words, it arises primarily and essentially from the gift and the effort of the individual. From this formal point of view, art can be as perfect in its earliest creators as in those who are to come, and further it unceasingly demands fundamental renewal.

PSEUDO-HYLAS. So that there is no reason why there should be necessary progress in the order of art.[43]

THEONAS. It is quite otherwise with the *speculative* order, the order of knowledge : here there is no question of operating in a matter, but of bringing truth into the soul : here matter, clothed by knowledge with an immaterial mode of being, is subjected to the conditions of the spirit. And as the amplitude of the spirit is boundless, so that one truth does not push out another but is joined to it, it is the law of growth which, in knowledge as such, will always tend to predominate.

Likewise knowledge, because it requires essentially the right ordination of concepts, and because the *via disciplinæ*, the intellectual transmission of the good that is acquired, plays the principal part—knowledge, then, human knowledge in its most formal aspect, demands tradition and teaching as a necessary condition of its growth. Therefore it is not to change, to the law of the other as other, that it is primarily submitted : but to progress, to the law of augmentation and movement towards perfection.

Thus we may understand why, despite accidental failings, the mathematical sciences—which of all sciences are best proportioned to the human mind—present an admirable example of progressive development : but we must note that even their progress normally involves revolution—though not destructive, but fertile, such as the invention of the infinitesimal method : their progress involves revolution because their object, the *ens quantum*, remains necessarily bound up with material things as perceived by the imagination, is in consequence not a pure intelligible, and so admits a certain multiplicity : this involves a possibility of renewal, as regards the primary conditions under which it comes under the grasp of the intelligence. And better than any other, it allows discoveries by the genius of the individual precisely because it is placed mid-way between the *being as changeable* of the natural philosopher—too closely bound up with matter—and the *being as being* of the metaphysician—too much abstracted from matter—and it is therefore most within the grasp of our mind and most within the power of our reason to handle.

We see the same history of progress—even, may be, more strikingly—since the time of Galileo in the physico-mathematical sciences—that is to say in the art of translating sensible phenomena into quantitative symbols : and this is precisely because those studies are in truth the poorest of all in intelligibility, the least exacting in intellectuality, hence the easiest. And in them there are the same revolutions, only more frequent still, because the theories proposed to the mind are not measured in the mind directly by the real, but only by their aptitude to support the network of mathematical formulations verified by experiment.

What now of metaphysics ? As it is the noblest science and has the most purely intelligible object—being as such —it is in metaphysics that the part played by the accidental is most restricted. Therefore it follows, with a minimum of upheavals and crises, what we have just seen to be the law of science as such—the law of continuous progress. In it, better than in any other, is realised the absolutely essential condition of this progress, namely, fixity of principles and stability of tradition : it does not require, for the discovery of its principles, extraordinary instruments and extraordinary conditions of research, but only the simplest evidence of the senses—used, it is true, by the purest intelligence. Consequently its foundations might well have been laid very early and, in fact, they were so laid. To repeat, then, in it is realised the absolutely essential condition of continuous progress, and therefore more than all other sciences it resembles, by the constancy of direction of its movement, the motionlessness of angelic knowledge.

Such, in fact, in spite of the enormous deficiencies of the human subject, is the eternal movement of metaphysics. In certain ages it experiences a slowing down, and even long intervals of stagnation, but it always resumes its flight in a direction that does not vary. You may say that, after all, its progress, save at a few luminous points of history, does not seem very rapid : I reply that by its imperceptible additions of new things to old, it has built up a treasury of wisdom not to be exhausted, in which the modern mind, formed and tempered by the progress of the individual sciences and so many painful experiences, may find a source of universal renewal. Metaphysics is most certainly the Queen of Sciences : it must, therefore, be magnanimous, and you know that Aristotle said that the magnanimous man advances slowly : *motus lentus magnanimi videtur, et vox gravis, et locutio stabilis ; est otiosus et tardus, utitur ironia, ad alios non potest convivere.*

Remember, too, that metaphysics is supremely difficult, by reason of its object which, being purely immaterial, is, to our reason, " as light to the eye of an owl." It follows that it must be the part of a very small number, and that there are moments when the deposit of wisdom could be transmitted only by the very slenderest spiritual thread. It follows also that philosophy is something other than the immense mass of the notions of philosophers, and that if all mathematicians co-operate in the growth of mathematics, and all scientists in the growth of science, all philosophers do not co-operate—at any rate directly—in the growth of philosophy. When they go wrong on principles, the direct effect of their work is towards the deterioration of philosophy ; and thus, while the law of progress dominates the eternal metaphysics of the human intellect, the law of pure change, of alteration and corruption, the tyranny of the other as such, the appetite for change proper to matter, constantly intervenes to frustrate philosophical effort outside the spiritual organism of philosophy scientifically formed.

Unless I am greatly deceived, my dear Sirs, all these somewhat austere considerations are not without their utility, for anyone who would see clearly into the questions of progress. One conclusion emerges from them : if in our day the Myth of Necessary Progress still seduces certain minds, one reason is that being heirs of an age hostile to all hierarchies and distinctions, we too often confuse different planes of the energies of man, bundling together in one single vague image the most diverse activities, and making a general law of what is true only in certain special cases.

SYSTEM OF
PHILOSOPHIC HARMONIES

SYSTEM OF PHILOSOPHIC HARMONIES

WE parted from Theonas and took our places in one of those suburban train compartments which break up in so brutally intellectualist a way the continuity of travellers. Both of us felt that sort of Pantheistic appeasement which goes with the end of a day in the country, when man relaxes his weary self in the scents of evening and of railway stations. But the grateful silence was soon broken by Philonous who suddenly asked :

" What then *is* this philosophy whose stability and non-revolutionary progress Theonas was boasting about ? Is it an ideal Metaphysics, a Platonic abstraction ? Or was he alluding to some actually existent system ? "

PSEUDO-HYLAS. I suppose he had in mind what we call, using a phrase of Leibnitz, the *philosophia perennis*, a philosophy implicitly contained in the certitudes of common-sense, given scientific form by Aristotle and further developed by St. Thomas Aquinas.

PHILONOUS. I should like to know of the progress this philosophy has made since the thirteenth century.

PSEUDO-HYLAS. For that we must turn to the school left by St. Thomas. It counted very great names in the sixteenth and seventeenth centuries : Cajetan was a contemporary of Luther, John of St. Thomas was a contemporary of Descartes ; the Carmelites of Salamanca were writing towards the end of the seventeenth century. It is said that a living thought is an evolving thought. This is a flat enough *cliché* : but it becomes the statement of a primary truth if the evolution in question is taken to mean not change but a development in doctrine. Vegetable and animal organisms stiffen and die, because they are material. But a living thought has never reached the term of its growth. So I am persuaded that in the great Thomists the thought of the master does not petrify, but develops, becomes a living being more perfect, more highly evolved. That is a truth not grasped by many intellectuals, victims of a romantic, and oh ! so easy, contempt for the Commentators.

PHILONOUS. Then, for you the progress of philosophy from the thirteenth century on, means simply such developments as the Aristotelianism of St. Thomas received from age to age at the hands of the scholastics or rather the Thomists, the purest of the pure, such as Capreolus, Cajetan, Bañes and other glories ! You please me singularly : you touch my heart with your beautiful candour. In the immense multitude of thinkers who have set their imprint on the modern consciousness, your eye picks out a handful of grim-visaged Dominicans and a handful of heavy-calibred Carmelites, buried in the folios of Vives. And you range yourself by their side : with them alone, against the world ! May I laugh ?

PSEUDO-HYLAS. Laugh by all means. I love to make you happy. But what of you ? If truth were hidden in the dusty decay of an old sarcophagus—the brain of M. Guignebert, for example—and it were necessary to bite

one's way in to get at it, would you not dash in enthusiastically ?   Seriously, I find you hard to please.   When
we defend the metaphysical value of common-sense and
choose for our masters, an Aristotle and a St. Thomas—
when we fall into the line of a spiritual tradition greater
than we at every point—you are not satisfied : you make
jokes about our simplicity, our sheeplike discipline, our
taste for what you call ironically the natural philosophy
of the human intellect—in short your accusation is that
we are in agreement with the human race.   But when we
refuse to join the dance of the *new—newer—newest* philosophy—wherein we should have the consolation of
believing in nobody, and getting on with everybody—
you are not satisfied either : you make jokes about our
insularity : your accusation is that we are alone in our
opinion—save for a handful of famous mendicants whose
principal crime is never to have been read by you.
Cantavimus vobis, et non saltastis ; lamentavimus, et non
planxistis.   Do not begrudge us the things we prize—an
intellectual love of the best taught us by all the sages, and
of a discipline humbly acquired, by virtue of which we
may look out from a high place upon the modern world.
" Mere variety of things known," as Heraclitus said long
ago, " does not constitute mind. . . . Thousands of
[merely learned men] do not counterbalance one single
excellent master . . . "   " If you do not expect the
unexpected," he said at another time, " you will not
attain truth, which is difficult to discern, hard of access."

Further, if truth is thus difficult of achievement, at
least in the highest matters, it is *a priori* much more likely
that it will be found in a condition of things differing
widely from the one we see about us—a roaring confusion

with every man setting his adolescent biceps to the remaking of the world (Descartes, Spinoza, Berkeley, Hume, Comte, Schopenhauer were under twenty-five when they forged the Idea of their universe) and with new planets incessantly hurled into space and endlessly colliding.

PHILONOUS. Your contempt for the greatest thinkers grates on me.

PSEUDO-HYLAS. You are quite wrong there : we have contempt for no one. Contempt we leave to those learned historians who—in the phrase used by Thomas in his Eulogy of Descartes—" from Aristotle to Descartes see a void of two thousand years." We, on the other hand, devote the most serious attention to the thought of every philosopher, even such as Holbach and Haeckel and Durkheim—doing our uttermost to find the living germ, mindful of the word of Scripture, *homines et jumenta salvabis Domine.* We sympathise with their effort——

PHILONOUS. Surely not. Is it not your conviction that since Descartes modern philosophy advances to the discovery of new aspects of the true only by way of errors whose inner logic tends of itself to the death of the reason ?

PSEUDO-HYLAS. Surely no other opinion is tenable.

PHILONOUS. And yet you talk of sympathy ! Ask M. Le Roy what it means to sympathise with modern philosophy : it means to embrace its varied curves, prolong within one-self its inner impulses. I see in my mind the philosophy, truly worthy of the name, which one day, as

I hope, will bring to pass the sacred union of the Spirit. Its thought—flexible and all-embracing, unformulated, incapable of formulation, untainted by any solidity of content, invertebrate as a jellyfish, fluid as water—will flow through all systems, adhering to none ; with equal certitude it will feel that all are true *in the making*, all false once they are made ; or rather it will be immersed in the stream of becoming far deeper than the stupid distinction between true and false. How absurd to think there is any question for a philosopher of being wrong or right ! Pulsations, vibrations, hidden tremblings—the enjoyment of these in all profundity will be its fulfilment. And since —as the common knowledge is at the Sorbonne—internal contradiction is the true sign of vitality, it will be by abandoning itself to, and savouring the delights of, contradiction in its uttermost multiplicity, that this thought, truly free, will feel the fecund vitality of modern philosophy and have ineffable communion with its essence, which is one sole movement in moments without number.

You, on the contrary, my poor friend, give yourself over bound hand and foot to the belief, set down by M. Parodi, " that Catholic philosophy has no need to follow the evolution of modern thought, and that it can without anxiety remain aside from all the ideas of our time."

PSEUDO-HYLAS. A German reviewer has written in the same sense : that I defend " a hyper-conservative Thomism " and that in my eyes the history of philosophy and the list of problems to be solved closed with the thirteenth century. That sort of thing is of course mere childishness, without malice but too facile. Since the occasion arises, I shall go into the accusation with you.

When two doctrines meet, opposed in spirit, and logically irreconcilable in their principles, what would you have them do, oh sensible Philonous, save seek to devour each other ? One *must* consume the other, not for the pleasure of destroying it, but for its own nourishment and the maintenance of its own life. There is nothing so ferocious as pure thought. In claiming to set yourself above logic and the principle of contradiction, and to efface from doctrines all specific determination and all that the mind can lay hold of, in order that you may take pleasure in their mere becoming—it is their very soul that you are suppressing, making their spiritual principle into a thing inanimate, non-living, formless ; for in every living thing the soul is that principle in the being which *determines* and *specifies*. I imagine you will grant me that the *soul* of a doctrine is its spirit and its principles. What you fail to perceive, so soundingly do the words " spirit " and " life " fill your mouth, is that you are reducing intellectual life to the conditions of pure matter and that by the strangest regression you are driving the word spirit back and back along the whole line of its historical development to a point where it signifies a sort of wind or breath giving rise in you to some formless surge of feeling that you mistake for thought.

PHILONOUS. What follows from that ?

PSEUDO-HYLAS. It follows that the true problem is quite simply the problem of organic assimilation. In every case of assimilation in which the *ego* nourishes its substance with *non-ego*, with things not itself, these cease to be what they are and become part of the *ego* : in other words, the *ego*, that it may enrich itself with all the virtualities of their matter, compels them to lose their own and receive its specifying principle—what we call its form.

It is not surprising then that a living philosophy should resist as a contamination and a corruption any kind of intrusion and commingling of a different " form "—all the more violently in proportion to the strength of its own living principle. Now the *philosophia perennis* is a living philosophy, claims to make us alive with a life which is above time, for it is truth. And we should not be living men but dead men if we did not reject the formal determinations in which is expressed the spirit of division, of anthropocentrism, of refusal to submit to the object, with which as we think " modern " philosophy is affected : if we did not see that the goal it has chosen as its term is quite simply the effort to make man a self-existent being, possessed of that absolute independence which belongs to God alone.

But, looking at it another way, it is clear that if a doctrine would live among men, it must constantly be assimilating what is other than itself and what is new : for that, it must remain in contact and, as it were, in continuity on the *material* side with all that is not itself ; and the stronger the spiritual principle that animates it, the more able it is to assimilate and integrate all things whatsoever. It would be a mortal sin to isolate truth in a lazar-house of sloth. And I grant you that scholastic philosophers have often committed this sin, a sin to which the professor and the pedagogue are peculiarly liable. But they have paid for it, and I think that to-day they make no mistake about the duty incumbent upon them of following with attention the new formation of ideas, and of re-thinking—according to the proper mode of their being, of course—all the problems of their time.

PHILONOUS. Very well—I agree that you do not avoid contact with modern philosophy. But it is only on the material side that you are willing to receive anything from it, or have communication with it. This seems to me a very penurious sort of contact.

PSEUDO-HYLAS. On the contrary, it is perfectly enormous ! for material contributions play an incalculable part in the development of human thought. What is important to us in the multitude of philosophic systems which have come treading upon one another's heels the last three hundred years is not only the sometimes excellent materials which they bring to light, but also their very errors : for these errors—by the boldness of their movement, by their logical repercussions and their interlinkings, by the splendour of the failure of such as Spinoza or Nietzsche—serve to bring into the most dazzling light the virtue of the principles and the inner springs of right philosophy. Important, also, in all these systems is the *desire* for truth which sets so many philosophers in the direction of a goal which they cannot attain—Comte, for instance, seeks the realisation of human order, Kant, the restoration of the activity of the subject in knowledge, Bergson, recognition of spiritual realities ; and again there are the *transpositions* of truth which they sometimes bring about, as when Leibnitz applies to our material universe many views which are true of the angelic world. And beyond all that is the refinement, the flexibility, the enrichment brought to our philosophic sensibility by modern philosophy.

All this, my dear Philonous, gives us much reason for a broad sympathy with the spiritual effort of the moderns, to say nothing of the sympathy we can feel with them as human beings if not always with them as themselves : for if it is absurd to treat philosophy, which is a science, as a " subjective poem," yet we can, and we must, look with admiration upon the history of the men who make philosophy, as upon a great drama.

Such are the thoughts which I had the honour of setting out more fully some time ago in the noble university of Louvain which has done so much for the Scholastic Revival and which far from being without doors or windows looking upon the outer world, has always taken so wide an interest in the concerns of the day. Thus you see we do not condemn everything *en bloc*, as you, with a touch of naïveté, seem to imagine ; on the contrary, we set ourselves, following the precept of the old logicians, to distinguish and divide.

PHILONOUS. A thankless job, for no one will want to follow you and you will find it difficult to maintain unvarying precision.

PSEUDO-HYLAS. I know. Nothing is more necessary to man than to *discern*, and nothing does he find more difficult. Ordinarily we work with intellectual instruments that we have not taken the trouble to sharpen, we use steam-hammers to crush a fly, and telegraph posts to mount a butterfly ; and we bring the paws of bears to the task of following out and drawing apart the threads of a spider's web.

PHILONOUS. Pascal, I think, said something similar—though with a less luxurious spread of metaphor.

PSEUDO-HYLAS. Yes. What he said was : "Justice and truth are two points so fine that our instruments are too blunt exactly to touch them. If they do arrive at them, they totally hide the point and rest on what lies around it—and more on the false than on the true." The only remedy is that man should learn the art of making right distinctions. That is one reason why philosophical studies, even when they do nothing but teach us this art, are of so vital a utility for the general government of our opinions ! Yet it would be a good thing that we should seek to imitate in our knowledge, according to our imperfect mode, the marvellous precision with which the divine action permeates the created thing without sharing its deficiencies—running through the most tenuous fibres, nerves, ducts, veinules of being.

At that moment a crowd of schoolgirls poured into our compartment, and our conversation could not maintain its slender existence against theirs. But soon Philonous, drawing up closer, went on in a low voice, "Your explanations do not yet satisfy me fully. In spite of all you say, the impression remains that, at a given moment and a given man, you bring to a full stop the development of philosophy : yet your master, St. Thomas said : ' *inventum philosophicum semper perfectibile.*' "

PSEUDO-HYLAS. And how could I be in doubt of a

truth so evident ? I make no claim that the development
of philosophy ceased at Aristotle or St. Thomas. I
believe only that their principles are true and that these
principles radiate in all directions throughout the real,
so that every *new* truth will, of necessity, be in agreement
with them and will find itself at home in Thomism. As
I think, the thing that came to a stop in Aristotle was not
the development of philosophy but the genesis of the
embryo, the *formation* of philosophy : so that after
Aristotle, philosophy, being formed, could henceforth
develop without end.

PHILONOUS. It seems to me also that you fail to grasp
not only that diversity of doctrines is legitimate, but also
that it is salutary and even indispensable ; and your
design is to reduce the intellect to a unity which I should
call a despotism. Look about you at all these young
faces : representing in every sort of fortunate or un-
fortunate combination the variety of " planetary types "
spoken of by Eugene Ledos. Surely you would not say
that an evil genius has taken pleasure in distorting them—
in puffing out some and collapsing others ! I am sure
that you prefer their diversity—the mingling of the more
agreeable and the less—to the monotony of one single
type repeated to infinity. Our conceptions and our
systems though they be true and founded in being, are
yet never so exhaustive that they exclude other complementary aspects logically irreconcilable. You make of
philosophic wisdom a science, a notional system, which,
in its logical interweaving, fully suffices to itself ; but I
am afraid that your intellectualism thereby fails to hold
many living germs scattered in the thought of man—

even, who knows, in the thought of St. Thomas himself and his masters. Leibnitz had a truer sense of the necessary multiplicity.

PSEUDO-HYLAS. That is an extremely specious objection.

PHILONOUS. I dare say you find in it a distant echo of my earlier conversations with a philosopher whose doctrine you do not approve, though you hold his character and intellect in high esteem . . .

PSEUDO-HYLAS. You mean M. Maurice Blondel ?

PHILONOUS. Exactly.

PSEUDO-HYLAS. I shall answer you very carefully. First of all, allow me to recall to your mind an ancient distinction which plays a leading rôle among scholastics— the distinction between *form* and the *subject* which it determines and which sustains, represents and often betrays it. That diversity of doctrines in which you and Leibnitz take such delight is necessary, not by reason of philosophy itself, but only by reason of the human subject and its infirmity—by reason, that is, of philosophers. Grant that a particular metaphysical doctrine is true—as in my eyes Thomism is true : given the weakness and limitations of the human intellect, it is safe to bet there are many aspects of truth which the philosophers attached to this true doctrine would fail to bring into relief if they, and they only, were pursuing the study of philosophy ; and it may happen that these neglected aspects of truth may find themselves brought clearly into light in certain otherwise erroneous doctrines—for every error affirms some truth. Thus a defect incidental and not essential in the one philosophy, is compensated by an excellence, likewise incidental and not essential, in the other : and the lucky discoveries of the sons of the foreign woman are as the measure of the omissions of the Children of Israel.

This way of looking at things finds singularly powerful confirmation in history which, from age to age, shows us the laziness, narrowness and incompetence of a great many of the pillars of truth. Nor need we be surprised at what is no more than an effect of the infirmity that belongs to the nature of man.

But if we are considering not the philosophers, but philosophy itself, then I cannot understand how you should consider multiplicity of doctrines necessary. If a metaphysic is true, all complementary aspects of truth, however diverse and heterogeneous, must, of necessity, be logically reconcilable with its principles ; and an intellect sufficiently penetrating, and sufficiently open to the real, must be able to discern these complementary aspects of truth without the incidental assistance of the teachers of error. To hold the contrary would be to conclude that there is a radical inequality between the intellect and being, to admit that reality is illogical fundamentally—that necessities for thought are not necessities for being—in short, one way or another to yield to the Kantian or post-Kantian blandishments and ruin intellectual knowledge.

PHILONOUS. All this assumes that philosophy is a

science, and that is precisely the point we refuse to concede.

PSEUDO-HYLAS. Yet you grant that philosophy is not totally imprisoned in doubt and in the appearances of things, and that it can procure us certitudes of real value ?

PHILONOUS. Certainly : that is why I am a philosopher and not a boxer or a stamp-collector ; but, for me, the certitudes of philosophy are not of the same order as the certitudes of science, and the intellect alone is not enough.

PSEUDO-HYLAS. Yet philosophy does not propose as its end the production of a work, as art does ? Nor does it propose as its end, like prudence, to set us to a right use of our freedom ?

PHILONOUS. No, its sole end is to know.

PSEUDO-HYLAS. It is clear that the certitudes of art and prudence presuppose—though on very different grounds [44]—a certain rectitude of the will, and that in these spheres the intellect alone does not suffice for right judgment, because it is working upon an object disproportioned to itself, and disproportioned by defect—I mean that it is working on a matter essentially contingent and particular, whereas the true object of the intellect is the necessary and the universal ; but I do not see how it can be the same for the certitudes of philosophy : for in philosophy the intellect *is* working on its proper object, on necessary and universal natures and laws, on being itself, with which it is its very nature to conform.

PHILONOUS. Yet may it not be that the first principles of being and the spiritual world are likewise disproportioned to the human intellect, not by defect, but by excess—with the result that it is incapable of attaining them without the aid of love, of the will, of the virtues which rectify and control action ?

PSEUDO-HYLAS. No. These first principles of being are disproportioned to the *direct apprehension* of the intellect, the sole object " connatural " to it being the nature of material things : that is why Aristotle held metaphysics to be a science properly divine. Yet it can know them by analogy, in the mirror of the sensible : for if as human it is inferior and limited, yet as intellect it must remain in some manner open to the infinity of being. Besides, if the supreme realities were beyond the reach of our intellect, what help could the will bring, since the will is on the same plane as the intellect ?

PHILONOUS. Yet did not Theonas remind us one day that our theologians said that there is a metaphysical wisdom which goes beyond the intellect in the knowledge of God, and that it does so by the aid of Charity ?

PSEUDO-HYLAS. Assuredly. But they also say that this wisdom which makes us " suffer—*pati*—rather than apprehend divine things," and which they number among the gifts of the Holy Ghost, is altogether of the supernatural order. Not only does it bear upon God according to His essence and His inmost life, in the secrets of His Deity, to which revelation alone can introduce us, but also it causes us to know Him according to an experimental mode which is of the super-human order. That is why it presupposes Charity, for it is by Charity that we are lifted on to the plane of the things of God. And do not forget that the gift in question resides in the intellect, and that as well as Charity it presupposes Faith—the principle and root of all the supernatural virtues, giving to our intellect the power to see all things *quasi oculo Dei*, without which there would be no love of God in the will.

It remains that in the natural order, reason cannot have recourse to the will to acquire a knowledge of the absolute of which it would be incapable by itself. On the contrary all that falls under the concept of being—including the ultimate principles and God Himself, regarded as causes of created things—must also be, more or less perfectly, accessible to our intellect : and so it may be the object of the intellect's certitudes without the help of any other faculty. Otherwise we should have, as I said a while ago, to conclude that there is a fundamental inequality between intellect and being.

PHILONOUS. Yet Plato thought that one must philosophise with one's whole soul.

PSEUDO-HYLAS. In so far as the impulse of the whole soul towards the truth and the purification of the will facilitate the exercise of pure intellect by removing those things which would be a hindrance to it, it is obviously necessary to philosophise with one's whole soul. But this phrase is utterly pernicious if it is used to mean that in the work of philosophy itself anything whatsoever must intervene other than pure intellect. Philosophy is, in fact, a body of certitudes exclusively intellectual, gathered solely as true—and not as good or desirable—and that is its only ground. This is no more than to say that it is properly a science, and that it draws its whole strength from the intuition of principles and from demonstration.

Its certitudes are not of the same order as the certitudes of science, if by the word science you mean the particular sciences which study the detail of secondary causes and derived truths—if, in fact, you mean by science what the moderns mean, namely systems of symbols directed towards the practical, or collections of particular facts and more or less probable opinions. But if you reserve the name of science, as in the fine Aristotelian acceptation, to that perfect intellectual knowledge which fixes the mind in the absolute stability of necessary truths, then you must say that the certitudes of philosophy are the certitudes of science *par excellence*—certitudes to which we attain only with the utmost difficulty.

How could it be otherwise, given that metaphysics is, among all the sorts of knowledge within the reach of our natural reason, the one that is at the summit of intellectuality? That is why, considering in unity the first truth and the ultimate principles, it towers over all the inferior sciences precisely as *wisdom*—not wisdom by way of instinct or inclination like that Wisdom which is a gift of the Holy Ghost—but wisdom by way of knowledge— scientific wisdom.[45] A striking sign of the depths to which the intellect has fallen in our day is the tendency of many fine minds to look upon philosophy as a sort of superior and cultured dreaming, in which every man, according to his own taste, expresses his individual personality and experience in certain views upon the world. The same fine minds usually proclaim the necessity of a return to philosophic culture ; and they do not see that if philosophy is not a science, and in its nature the supreme science, it is nothing at all.

But if philosophy is a science, since all science is, of itself, infallible, we must conclude that there are not several philosophies, but only one, and that the infinity of philosophic errors—like the multiplicity of doctrines and such utility as we have seen this multiplicity can have —are the work of philosophers, not of philosophy. Here we are back again at that distinction between *form* and *subject* with which I began. This distinction is of capital importance and the failure to grasp it is the root of a horde of errors. It would be imprudent to judge philosophy by philosophers, art by artists, the ideal by idealists, order by officials, and piety by the pious !

It seems to me that if you saw this distinction in all its bearings, you would understand our position better : you would see how we stand for unity by reason of the form, yet allow for diversity by reason of the matter or the subject.

We aspire to the unity of the intellect—who, indeed, would choose the multiple as his end ? Does not unity go with truth and with being ? But it is not a despotic unity, for it may be procured only by integration in light. And we know well enough that it will never find complete realisation among men. If we deplore the errors bound up with diversity of doctrines and refuse to admit them in God the Author of truth—yet on the other hand we rejoice in the diversity in the human subject, we love to find it in God the Author of nature and of the universal order. We are prepared to agree with you that philosophy is fully self-sufficient, *in itself*, in the framework that belongs to it ideally—that is, it is capable of receiving all the immensity of the real within the immaterial web of its principles. But regarded not in itself, but only in the subjects wherein it dwells—in the men who profess it and represent it, and in this or that moment of human history —philosophy as an organism scientifically constituted, the *philosophia perennis* which is always in progress, does undoubtedly leave outside its actually defined and formulated framework many truths which its own principles are *in fact* especially adapted to bring to light and which must put up with the shelter of false systems for a time.

It is these partial truths, these vital elements, these scattered aspects of beauty—which sometimes stand out in extraordinary relief in the false light and the crude perspective of erroneous doctrines—it is these that we must gather and save, with the care which a philosophy worthy of the name must have for all that is. These are the true food which right philosophy must assimilate. Thomism has fasted this three hundred years. The history of modern philosophy has prepared certain tasty dishes for the breaking of its fast.

It is only now, it seems to me, that I have answered the question you put me when we left Theonas as to the progress of philosophy. This progress does not concern only the acquisitions of truth within the body of the *philosophia perennis :* it concerns also truths accidentally or virtually attained outside. It includes not only the actual gains that Philosophy has made, but also its virtual gains which fall to us as of right : for all is ours if we are Christ's.

You see, my friend, that our method is not Omar's method, and that we too can construct—without falling short of the duty we owe to truth—a system of philosophic harmonies. Likewise you see that while we admit as a fact—and a fact of very great gravity—the general weakening of the intellect in modern times, yet we do not, therefore, profess—as do the esotericism and pure traditionalism of the East—the absolute immobility of metaphysics. As a human science, philosophy must progress with time, and I have just told you the very definite sense in which we understand this progress. Yet I wish you could have grasped that the Myth of necessary Progress is the most powerful obstacle to the real progress which philosophy is in fact making : for the Myth implies that the modern must continually displace and reject the old, imposes chronology upon truth as a criterion, and makes of the category " out of date " a scarecrow for thought.

We were drawing near to Paris. Philonous rose, looking for his umbrella in the rack. " Do you know," he said, " that I have decided to sail for America ? . . . I should like to take with me on the boat a few books dealing with the origins and the development of this idea of Progress of which we have spoken—since we have spoken of it rather as philosophers than as historians."

" It is," I answered, " quite a modern idea ; it made its first appearance in the seventeenth century, and was spread among the public by the quarrel between the Ancients and the Moderns. I have made some little study of its history. To understand its repeated successes, it is necessary to realise many things : the almost exclusive ascendancy exercised from the seventeenth century onwards by the positive sciences and their applications :

the influence of Descartes who was responsible for the rupture of the modern intellect with the past : then in the eighteenth century, optimism and the relative intellectual inferiority of the salons : the intellectual Societies with their endless debating and the inevitable production of myths and pseudo-ideas which followed upon it : the naturalist degradation and the Masonic counterfeit of Christian ideas to which Theonas alluded today : and lastly to the evolutionist metaphysics which lay as a cloud over the nineteenth century. On all this you will find much information and many useful comments made from different points of view in Georges Sorel's *Illusions du Progrès*, René Loti's book *Du Christianisme au Germanisme*, Augustin Cochin's book on *Les Sociétés de Pensée et la Démocratie*, and the *Essays on the Idea of Progress* by the English writers Professor Bury, who was very much in love with the idea, and Dean Inge, who has no illusions about it at all. But what are you going to do in America ? "

" Paris—Denfert ! " shouted the porters.

Philonous bustled out of the carriage and his answer was lost in the uproar.

NOTES

NOTES

1. St. Gregory the Great, *in Job*, xxvii, 21, *Moral.*, lib. XVIII, cap. 54. *More suo (Paulus) homines (vocat) omnes humana sapientes, quia qui divina sapiunt videlicet suprahomines sunt.* As *videlicet*, put there to introduce an unaccustomed word, indicates, *suprahomines* is here a compound and must be written as one word, as in the *Liber Sententiarum* of Taion (I, 37), edited by Risco (*España Sagrada*, t. XXXI, 152 *sqq.*), where this passage of St. Gregory is reproduced. St. Gregory insists upon the idea : *Videbimus igitur Deum, si per coelestem conversationem* suprahomines *esse mereamur.* (*Ibid.*)

2. Cf. Aristotle, *Politics*, III, 13.

3. Henri Bergson, *La Perception du Changement*, Oxford and London, Henry Frowde, 1911, p. 27.

4. Noel Vesper, *Anticipations à une morale du risque. Essai sur la malléabilité du monde*, Paris, Perrin, 1914. The work quoted is a youthful essay ; since then M. Vesper has developed his thought in a different direction, much more solidly rational. Among the French Protestant *élite*, he is one of those whose reflections deserve to be followed with greatest attention.

5. Cassian, *Conf.*, XXIII, c. 3.

6. Clerissac, *Le Mystère de l'Eglise*, 3e ed., 1925.

7. Albert Einstein, *Uber die spezielle und die allgemeine Relativitätstheorie*, 5th ed., Wieweg, Braunschweig, 1920.

8. Aristotle, *Phys.*, lib. IV, c. 11, n. 5. I wished, in this second edition (1925), to dwell especially upon the exposition of the Aristotelico-Thomist doctrine upon time ; hence I

decided to develop it more technically, with the addition of numerous notes.

For a discussion of the Einsteinian theory of time and relativity, see ch. VII of my *Réflexions sur l'intelligence*.

9. These successive *befores* and *afters* are thus caused in movement by the *befores* and *afters* of the extension traversed. Thus they can enter into the definition of time without any vicious circle. (H. Carteron, in his interesting *Remarques sur la notion du temps d'après Aristote*, Revue Philosophique, Jul.-Aug. 1924, might have brought this out more clearly). *Dicendum est quod prius et posterius ponuntur in definitione temporis, secundum quod causantur in motu ex magnitudine, et non secundum quod mensurantur ex tempore ; et ideo supra Aristoteles ostendit, quod prius et posterius prius sunt in magnitudine quam in motu, et in motu quam in tempore, ut haec objectio excludatur.* St. Thomas, *Comm. in Phys. Arist.*, lib. iv, lect. 17.

10. St. Augustine, *Conf.*, lib. II, c. 23.

11. St. Thomas Aquinas, *Comm. in Phys. Arist.*, lib. IV, lect. 17.

12. Cf. John of St. Thomas, *Curs. Phil.*, Phil. Nat., I. P., q. xviii, a. 2.

13. Aristotle, *Phys.*, lib. IV., c. 14, n. 3.

14. *Numerus dicitur dupliciter. Uno modo* id quod numeratur actu, vel quod est numerabile ; *utpote cum dicimus decem homines vel decem equos : qui dicitur* numerus numeratus. . . . *Alio modo dicitur numerus quo numeramus, id est ipse numerus absolute acceptus, ut duo, tria, quatuor. Tempus autem non est numerus quo numeramus . . . sed est numerus numeratus, quia ipse numerus prioris et posterioris in motu tempus dicitur : vel etiam ipsa quae sunt prius et posterius numerata.* St. Thomas, in *Phys. Arist.*, lib. IV, c. xi, lect. 17.

15. " *Est ergo dubitatio utrum non existente anima esset tempus, aut non.*

" *Ibi ' Impossibile enim ' :*

" *Objicit ad ostendendum quod non : quia si impossibile esset esse aliquod potens numerare, impossibile esset esse aliquod numerabile, potens scilicet numerari : sed, si non est numerabile, non est numerus, quia numerus non est nisi in eo quod numeratur actu vel quod est numerabile in potentia. Relinquitur ergo, quod si non est aliquod potens numerare, quod non sit numerus. Sed nihil aliud natum est numerare quam anima, et inter partes animae non alia quam intellectus : quia numerus fit per collationem numeratorum ad unam primam mensuram ; conferre autem rationis est. Si ergo non est anima intellectiva, non est numerus. Tempus autem est numerus, ut dictum est. Si ergo non sit anima intellectiva, non est tempus.*

" Ibi ' nisi hoc ' :

" Solvit dubitationem ; et dicit, quod aut oportet dicere quod tempus non sit, si non est anima, aut oportet hoc dicere verius, quod tempus est utcumque ens sine anima : utputa si contingit motum esse sine anima : sicut enim ponitur motus, ita necesse est poni tempus : quia prius et posterius in motu sunt, et haec, scilicet prius et posterius motus, in quantum sunt numerabilia, sunt ipsum tempus. Ad evidentiam autem hujus solutionis considerandum est quod positis rebus numeratis, necesse est poni numerum ; unde, sicut res numeratae dependent a numerante, ita et numerus earum, esse autem rerum numeratarum non dependet ab intellectu, nisi sit aliquis intellectus qui sit causa rerum, sicut est intellectus divinus ; non autem dependet ab intellectu animae ; unde nec numerus rerum ab intellectu animae dependet, sed solum ipsa numeratio, quae est actus animae, ab intellectu animae dependet. Sicuti ergo possunt esse sensibilia sensu non existente, ita possunt esse numerabilia et numerus non existente numerante.

" Sed forte conditionalis, quam primo posuit, est vera : scilicet quod, si est impossible *esse aliquem numerantem, impossibile est esse aliquod numerabile ; sicut haec est vera, si impossibile est esse aliquem sentientem, impossibile est esse aliquid sensibile. Si enim est sensibile, potest sentiri ; et si potest sentiri potest esse aliquod sentiens : licet non sequatur quod, si est sensibile, quod sit sentiens. Et similiter sequitur, quod si est aliquid numerabile, quod possit esse aliquid numerans : unde, si impossibile est esse aliquod numerans, impossibile est esse aliquid numerabile : non tamen sequitur, quod si non est numerans, quod non sit numerabile, ut objectio Philosophi procedebat.*

" Si ergo motus haberet esse fixum in rebus, sicut lapis vel equus, posset absolute dici, quod sicut etiam anima non existente est numerus lapidis, ita etiam anima non existente esset numerus motus, qui est tempus. Sed motus non habet esse fixum in rebus, nec aliquid actu invenitur in rebus de motu, nisi quoddam indivisibile motus, quod est

motus divisio : sed totalitas motus accipitur per considerationem animae, comparantis priorem dispositionem mobilis ad posteriorem. Sic igitur, et tempus non habet esse extra animam, nisi secundum suum indivisibile. Ipsa tamen totalitas temporis accipitur per ordinationem animae numerantis prius et posterius in motu, ut supra dictum est ; et ideo signanter dicit Philosophus quod tempus non existente anima est utcumque ens, id est imperfecte ; sicut et si dicatur quod motum contingit esse sine anima imperfecte. Et per hoc solvuntur rationes supra positae ad ostendendum quod tempus non sit, quia componitur ex partibus non existentibus : patet enim ex praedictis, quod non habet esse perfectum extra animam sicut nec motus." St. Thomas, *Comm. in Phys. Arist.*, lib. IV, lect. 23. Cf. John of St. Thomas, *loc. cit.*, a. 1, 2ª *difficultas ;* H. Carteron, *Remarques sur la notion du temps d'après Aristote, Revue philosophique*, Jul.-Aug. 1924 (p. 78) : " The mind then intervenes in time only in a secondary way, making of time an actual number—that is, providing a conventional and artificial determination (cf. Boethius, in *Themistius*, 163, 6)."

16. " *Relatio mensurae non est ipsum tempus, sed fundamentum hujus relationis.*" . . . (John of St. Thomas, *loc. cit.*). On this confusion of quantity and relation, cf. Roland Dalbiez, *Dimensions absolues et mesures absolues, Revue thomiste*, Mar.-April 1925.

17. All that there is of divisibility and continuity—hence of quantity in the proper sense of the word—in time, comes to it from movement. That is why it may be called a " quantity," but *per accidens* or rather *per posterius*. " *Tempus est divisibile et continuum propter motum ; motus autem propter magnitudinem ; non quidem propter magnitudinem ejus quod movetur, sed propter magnitudinem ejus in quo aliquid movetur. Ex eo enim quod illa magnitudo est quanta, et motus est quantus. Et propter hoc quod motus est quantus, sequitur tempus esse quantum. Unde haec (sc. motus et tempus) non solum per accidens quantitates dici possunt, sed magis per posterius, in quantum quantitatis divisionem ab aliquo priori sortiuntur.*" St. Thomas, *in Metaph. Arist.*, lib. V, lect. 15 (ed. Cathala, n. 985). Cf. John of St. Thomas, *Curs. Phil.*, Log. II. P., q. XVI, a. 3.

18. Aristotle, *Phys.*, lib. IV, c. x, n. 10 ; c. xii, n. 2, (St. Thomas, lect. 16 and 19).

19. St. Thomas, *in Metaph. Arist.*, lib. V, lect. 15, n. 986 ; in II *Sent.*, dist. 27, q. 1, a. 2, ad. 1 ; q. 1, *De Verit.*, a. 5.— John of St. Thomas, Phil. Nat., I. P., q. 18, a. 3. (p. 332 Vives).

20. Cf. St. Thomas Aquinas, *in Metaph. Arist.*, lib. V, c. xv, lect. 17 ; lib. X, lect. 2, n. 1956 *sqq ; Sum. theol.*, I–II, 90, 1 ; I, 10, a. 4, 5, 6 ; 14, 8, ad. 3, etc.

21. " *Ea mensurantur, quae accipiunt esse et specificationem ab alio.*" John of St. Thomas, *Curs. Phil.*, Log. II. P., q. XVII, a. 3. This is said of the measure which is the foundation of relations of the third kind (*quae dicitur mensura secundum commensurationem esse et veritatis*), and which as such is of another order than the thing measured. What is here called ontological measure is of this class.

Another class of measure is constituted by mathematical measure ; the relations corresponding to this belong to the first kind of relations (comparison of a geometrical collection or magnitude with a unit of the same order, and more generally comparison or contrast. Cf. St. Thomas, *in Metaph. Arist.*, lib. X, lect. 2, n. 1954).

The measure of physical magnitudes, whether it is taken in the philosopher's or the physicist's sense, participates in both classes at once, since on the one hand it implies quantitative comparison (relation of the first kind) and on the other it imposes upon physical reality a specification and a co-ordination, whether *really* (ontological measure, with real relation of the third kind) or *secundum rationem* (measure of the physicist, with ideal relation of the third kind). See below, n. 23.

22. Aristotle, *Metaph.*, lib. X, c. 1 (lect. 2 of St. Thomas, n. 1938).

23. In this case there is (1) *transcendental* real relation of our conventional units and our measuring instruments with the reality to be measured (for these units have been chosen and these instruments made only to measure this reality, and therefore transcendentally depend upon it) ; (2) *predicamental* real relation of the first kind (*secundum quantitatem seu proportionem, scilicet unitatem et numerum, convenientiam vel dis-*

convenientiam, etc.), otherwise called relation of measure or of mathematical comparison between our units and the quantity measured ; and (3) *predicamental* (pseudo-predicamental, for it is only *secundum rationem*) of the third class, that is relation of measure in the philosophical sense (*secundum commensurationem esse et veritatis*) between the reality measured and our units and measures, which determine and specify (for us) the quantity of the thing measured : a relation *which is not mutual* (in the relations of the third kind " *extrema non mutuo ordinantur sed unum tantum ordinatur ad aliud*," the thing measured being as such dependent upon the measure and not *vice versa*), and which imposes on the reality measured the domination of our measures, but which can only be *ens rationis*, since the reality measured, the quantity of things, does not depend really upon our measures. Thus our physical measures place in the reality measured a relation (*rationis*) of the third kind, such that the spatial and temporal dimensions of things depend (*secundum rationem*) upon our units. Hence the relativism of physico-mathematical science.

On the theory of relation and the three kinds of predicamental relations—*secundum proportionem, secundum actionem, secundum mensuram*—see Aristole, *Metaph.*, lib. V, c. xv (St. Thomas, lec. 17) ; and John of St. Thomas, *Curs. Phil.*, Log. II. P., q. XVII.

24. It is thus right to apply to measure the distinction, classic among the ancients (particularly in their theory of *propositiones per se notae*), of *secundum se* and *quoad nos*.

25. St. Thomas, *in Metaph. Arist.*, lib. X, c. 1, lect. 2, n. 1955.

26. Cf. John of St. Thomas, *Curs. Phil.*, Phil. Nat., I. P., q. XVIII, a. 3.

27. Kleutgen, *La Philosophie scolastique exposée et défendue*, t. II, Diss. IV, ch. IV, p. 138. It is to be noted that each of these proper or internal times is *uniform by definition ;* it is in effect measured by its own divisions, and these coincide precisely with those of the movement itself or the space covered by the thing in motion. Cf. John of St. Thomas, *Curs. Phil.*, Phil. Nat., I. P., q. XVIII, a. 1, 1ᵃ *difficultas ;* " *Si*

loquamur de tempore coeli respectu motuum inferiorum, quos extrinsece mensurat, clare constat, quod distinguatur ab aliis realiter. Si vero loquamur de tempore respectu motus, in quo est intrinsece, sic distinguitur, sicut duratio a re durante, quae in motu, cum successivus sit, not fit per continuationem ejusdem indivisibilis existentiae, sed per continuatam additionem unius partis ad aliam, ut dictum est. Et hac ratione motus dicitur durare pauco tempore, vel multo, non quidem respectu temporis ipsi motui intrinseci, hic enim motus in duratione adæquatur tempore sibi intrinseco, sed comparative ad tempus extrinsecum mensurans, ipsa autem duratio intrinseca motus non est major, nec minor, quam motus ipse.''

28. Cf. Cajetan, *in Sum. theol.*, I, 10, 6 : '' *Adverte hic, quod sicut quilibet motus habet proprium prius et posterius in seipso, ita etiam habet proprium numerum numeratum illorum : et consequenter proprium tempus : sed quoniam non cujuslibet motus numerus est certificativus omnium motuum ex natura sua, sed tantum numerus primi motus propter ejus simplicitatem maximam, ideo solus primi motus numerus temporis complete rationem habet. Et propterea tempus est unum numero formaliter completeque sumptum : et sunt multa tempora quasi materialiter seu incomplete.*''

29. This is what Pseudo-Hylas attempts to show § VII and VIII, p. 88 ff.

30. He who perceives any movement, existent either in sensible objects or in the soul, perceives being as transmutable, and by that very fact he perceives the first movement, cause of all others, with the time which is bound up with it [as its intrinsic measure, and as extrinsic measure of other movements]. And thus whoever perceives any movement at all, perceives time, though time is bound up with the first movement only, by which all others are caused and measured.'' St. Thomas, *in Phys. Arist.*, lib. VI, lect. 17 ; cf. *Sum. Theol.*, I, 10, 6 : '' *Est ergo ratio unitatis temporis unitas primi motus, secundum quem, cum sit simplicissimus, omnes alii mensurantur, ut dicitur in X. Metaph. Sic ergo tempus ad illum motum comparatur, non solum ut mensura ad mensuratum, sed etiam ut accidens ad subjectum ; et sic ab eo recipit unitatem. Ad alios autem motus comparatur solum ut mensura ad mensuratum. Unde secundum eorum*

multitudinem non multiplicatur : quia una mensura separata multa mensurari possunt."

It should be added that it there is no need to subject time and first movement within a particular *mobile* such as the first celestial sphere of the ancients. To safeguard what is formal in the notion of first movement, it is sufficient to link time with the simplest and most fundamental type of movement or change. (What this movement is, I neither know nor need to know.)

31. "*Ad hoc, quod aliqua mensurantur per aliquod unum, non requiritur, quod illud unum sit causa omnium eorum, sed quod sit simplicius.*" St. Thomas, *Sum. theol.*, I, 10, 6, ad 4.

32. St. Thomas, *Sum. theol.*, I, 10, 6 ; Cajetan, in I, 10, 5–6.

33. "*Sciendum enim est quod praedicatum ad subjectum tripliciter se potest habere. Uno modo cum est id quod est subjectum, ut cum dico : Socrates est animal. . . . Secundo modo ut praedicatum sumatur secundum quod inest subjecto ; quod quidem praedicatum,* vel inest ei PER SE ET ABSOLUTE, *ut consequens materiam,* et sic est QUANTITAS ; *vel est consequens formam, et sic est qualitas ; vel inest ei* NON ABSOLUTE, *sed in respectu ad aliud, et sic est* AD ALIQUID . . . " St. Thomas, in *Metaph. Arist.*, lib. V, c. VII, lect. 9, n. 891–892. Observe how clearly St. Thomas distinguishes quantity from relation and marks the absolute character of the former.

34. Cf. St. Thomas, *Sum. theol.*, I, 10, 6 ; *in Phys. Arist.*, lib. IV, lect 15 ; lect. 23 : "*Tempus primo mensurat et numerat primum motum circularem : et per eum mensurat omnes alios motus, unde est unum tempus tantum propter unitatem primi motus*" *;* in I *Sent.*, dist. 37, q. 4, a. 3 : "*Sed dico, quod tempus istud (sc. angeli) est aliud a tempore quo mensuratur motus coeli et aliorum corporalium : quod sic probatur. Nullus motus mensuratur per motum coeli nisi qui est ordinatus ad ipsum. Unde etiam probant philosophi, I de Coelo text. 90, quod si essent plures mundi, oporteret esse plures primos motus et plura tempora. Unde cum motus angeli nullum ordinem habeat ad motum coeli, et praecipue si motus ejus dicatur successio operationum, ut dictum est, oportet quod non mensuretur tempore quod est mensura primi mobilis, sed alio tempore, cujus temporis naturam ex natura motus accipere oportet. In tempore enim*

est aliquid quasi formale, quod tenet se ex parte quantitatis discretae, sc. numerus prioris et posterioris ; et aliquid materiale, per quod est continuum, quia continuitatem habet ex motu in quo est sicut in subjecto et primo mensurato, sc. motus coeli, ut dicitur IV Phys. text. 99. Motus autem ille habet continuitatem ex magnitudine." Sent. I, dist. 37, q. 4, a. 3, c.

35. Cf. St. Thomas, *in Phys. Arist.*, lib. IV, lect. 23, *sub fine.* St. Thomas, in this passage, does not envisage the hypothesis of a multiplicity of separate worlds. But he declares that if one left out of account the unity of the first movement (that is the unity of the world) one would have, in applying to different particular durations one same abstract number, a time " unum specie sed non numero."

Note that the times of diverse separate worlds would have the same specific nature since they would all be the duration of a continuous movement, that is time of a material world : whereas there is specific difference between the continuous time of matter and the " discontinuous time " which measures the operations of pure spirits.

36. St. Thomas, in I *Sent.*, dist. 19, q. 2, a. 1 ; *Sum. theol.*, I, 10, 2 ; Sanseverino, *Elementa Philosophiae christianae*, t. II, Ontologia, c. 7, a. 1 ; John of St. Thomas, *Curs. Phil.*, Phil. Nat., I. P., q. 18, a. 1 : " *Duratio in communi accepta nihil est aliud, quam persistentia in existendo. . . . In rebus permanentibus duratio non addit super existentiam aliquid intrinsecum, sed est idem cum existentia, et solum addit extrinsecam connotationem, et dependentiam ab actione continuante et influente ipsum esse ; in rebus autem successivis, quia duratio fit per novarum partium effluxum, consequenter duratio fit per superadditionem existentiae ad existentiam.*"

37. Cf. John of St. Thomas, Phil. Nat., *loc. cit.* ; Log., II. P., q. 16, a. 3 (Vivès, p. 488) ; H. Carteron, *Remarques sur la notion du temps d'après Aristote*, Revue philosophique, Jul.-Aug. 1924 : " In a general way (221 *a* 4–7 ; *b* 3–7 ; *b* 28–222 *a* 10) time penetrates things that move in such a way that it measures their existence but not things themselves, except movement."

38. Cf. St. Thomas, *Sum. theol.*, I, 10, a. 2 and 4 a. 5, ad 3 ;

14, a. 13 ; 53, a. 3 ; *opusc. de Instantibus*, cap. I : " *Una ergo particula indivisibilis illius temporis (sc. angelorum) manere potest cum multo tempore nostro, cujus tamen partes illi particulæ commanere non possunt.*" *De Verit.*, q. 2, a. 12 ; JOHN OF ST. THOMAS, *Curs. Phil.*, Phil. Nat., I. P., q. 18, a. 1, 3ᵃ diffic. *Manifestum est*, as Aristotle said, *quod non est idem esse in tempore, et esse quando tempus est.* (*Phys.*, lib. IV, cap. XII, n. 9. Lec. 20 OF ST. THOMAS.)

39. It is so because modern physics is an intermediate science, at once physics and mathematics—but *materially* physics and *formally* mathematics. Since formally it is mathematics, it is in itself, if not in its origins, independent of experience, with which its only link is by way of its application. Cf. my *Réflexions sur l'Intelligence*, ch. VI., and *Les Degrés du Savoir*, ch. II and IV.

40. In truth time itself, inasmuch as it is bound up essentially with movement, which in turn is essentially bound up with matter, tends towards dissolution, and all progress is, metaphysically, an effort to rise above time. This is a fundamental law of which ancient wisdom was not ignorant : " *Sed quidam Philosophus, Paro nomine, de secta Pythagoricorum, posuit e converso, videlicet, quod penitus tempus est indisciplinabile, quia scilicet per longitudinem temporis accidit oblivio. Et in hoc rectius dixit ; quia, ut supra dictum est, tempus per se magis est causa corruptionis quam generationis : et hoc ideo, quia tempus est numerus motus : mutatio autem per se est destructiva et corruptiva, sed causa generationis et ipsius esse non est nisi per accidens : ex hoc enim ipso quod aliquid movetur, recidet a dispositione quam prius habebat : sed quod perveniat ad aliquam dispositionem, hoc non importatur in ratione motus, in quantum est motus, sed in quantum est finitus et perfectus ; quam quidem perfectionem habet motus ex intentione agentis, quod movet ad determinatum finem.*" (ST. THOMAS, *in Phys. Aristotelis*, lib. IV, c. XIII, lect. 22.)

41. *Three Reformers*, ch. III.

42. LÉON LAFFITTE, Une définition du progrès, *Mercure de France*, Mar. 1, 1921.

43. In the volume of memoirs published by M. Ambrose

NOTES

Vollard on Renoir, I find certain reflexions of the great painter which I cannot resist the temptation to quote :

" RENOIR. Progress in painting I certainly do not admit. There is no progress in ideas, and none, therefore, in methods. One day I wanted to change my yellow : I messed about for ten years. In sum, the palette of our painters to-day remains the same as that of the painters of Pompeii, by way of Poussin, Corot and Cézanne : I mean that it has grown no richer. The ancients used earth, ochre, ivory black : with these anything can be done. Much effort has been spent to add a few tones : but how easily we could have done without them ! Thus, I have spoken to you of the great discovery that was thought to have been made by the substitution of blue and red for black ; but how far this combination is from giving the *finesse* of ivory black—which besides does not oblige the wretched painter to be looking for midday at two in the afternoon ! With their restricted palette, the old painters could do as well as to-day (we must be polite to our contemporaries) and certainly what they did had more solidity.

" I. But if the painter cannot, reasonably, dream of a new palette——

" RENOIR. What must be the supreme object of his effort ? It must be to affirm and perfect his craft : but it is only by tradition that this can be achieved. To-day we all have genius, of course : but what is certain is that we cannot draw a hand and know nothing of our craft. It was by possession of their craft that the ancients could attain that marvellous surface and those limpid colours whose secret we search for in vain. I am afraid that it is not by new theories that the secret will be revealed.

" But if workmanship is the basis and solid principle of art, it is not the whole. In the art of the ancients there is something else that makes their productions so beautiful—that serenity which is the reason why we never weary of looking at them, which suggests to us the eternal workmanship. This serenity they had within themselves, not only as an effect of their simple tranquil lives, but still more because of their religious faith. They were conscious of their weakness, and in their successes as well as in their failures, they associated God with their actions. God is always there, and man does not count. With the Greeks, it was Apollo or Minerva ; the painters of Giotto's day likewise chose a heavenly patron. It was thus that their works acquired that aspect of sweet serenity which gives them their profound charm and makes them immortal. But man, in his modern pride, chose to reject this collaboration, which diminished him in his own eyes. He cast out God, and so doing, cast out happiness. . . .

" The painters of those enviable ages had of course some defects—fortunately for them—but looking at their works, which have conserved so much freshness across the ages, we think only of their qualities. Those pictures that one loves to touch with the finger, like fine marbles, those marvellous surfaces, that divine workmanship fill me with joy. In France there was for centuries a fine rivalry in taste and fancy : châteaux spring from the soil : bronze, china, tapestry that look like the work of fairies : everyone co-operating—in earth, wood, iron, wool, marble—for the enrichment of France. To the end of the eighteenth century all was beauty, from the château to the humblest cottage. See the albums of the Trocadéro museum and get an idea of the strength of those artists, of the firmness of design in the tiniest details— a bolt, a door knob ! Those men were not working to exhibit at the Salon ! "

44. Art does not, like prudence, suppose a rectification of the appetite *in relation to the end of man*, or in the field of moral conduct. But it supposes a rectification of the appetite *in relation to the proper end of the art itself* (CAJETAN, in *Sum. theol.*, I–II, q. 117, *a*. 5, *ad*. 3). Cf. *Art and Scholasticism*, ch. VI.

45. *Scientia debet esse naturaliter aliarum regulatrix, quae maxime intellectualis est.* ST. THOMAS, *in Metaph. Aristot.*, procemium.

46. Here again mention must be made of the Russian philosopher, Nicholas Berdiaeff, who in his suggestive book, *Un Nouveau Moyen Age* (translated into English with the title *The End of Our Time*) shows very clearly the archaic and reactionary character of the myth of Progress.